"If there's a young man in your church who senses a call to pastoral ministry, give him this book. Likewise, give it to a seminary student you know or a man early in his pastoral ministry. There's a bounty of biblical teaching and practical advice condensed in these pages. Too many men in ministry, as was true for me, had to learn much of this the hard way: by years of experience and through many mistakes. My first years in the ministry would have gone much smoother for me and better for the people I pastored if I'd had the benefit of this book decades ago."

Dr. Donald S. Whitney, professor of biblical spirituality and associate dean at The Southern Baptist Theological Seminary, Louisville, Kentucky, and author of *Spiritual Disciplines for the Christian Life*, *Praying the Bible*, and *Family Worship*

"The call to be a pastor does not come with automatic insight, knowledge, or competency. Consequently, every shepherd sometimes finds himself overwhelmed, over-worked, underappreciated, and unprepared for the deluge of demands on his time and the constant drain on his spirit. That is precisely the moment when someone needs to put a copy of Jason Allen's *Letters to My Students* in his hands. Filled with biblical truth, practical wisdom, Christian warmth, and gentle instruction on every page, this book reads like an encouraging conversation with a trusted friend who knows what is needed to walk the pathway of joyful obedience."

Dr. Hershael York, dean of the School of Theology; Victor and Louise Lester Professor of Christian Preaching at The Southern Baptist Theological Seminary, Louisville, Kentucky, and senior pastor of Buck Run Baptist Church in Frankfort, Kentucky

"I am so thankful for *Letters to My Students* from Jason Allen. It might look like a book, but really it's an oppor-tunity. It's an opportunity to sit with and learn from a godly man who has dedicated his life to the ministry of

Jesus Christ, and to equipping others for that ministry. He knows the ministry priorities; and as he guides you through them he will help you see the pleasures and avoid some of the pain. You will be wiser and more prepared once you have heard from this man. I wish this has been available twenty-five years ago."

Dr. Heath Lambert, senior pastor of
First Baptist Church in Jacksonville, Florida

"This book is really good. Clear, concise, and packed with straightforward practical advice for every pastor. This volume will be especially helpful for those just getting started in pastoral ministry. If only I had this book thirty years ago! This book should be handed out to every seminary graduate in the country."

Dr. Clint Pressley, senior pastor of Hickory Grove
Baptist Church in Charlotte, North Carolina

"'For The Church' is not only the mantra of Dr. Jason Allen's vision for Midwestern Seminary, but it is also his life's passion. I cannot think of a better person to share wisdom about pastoring than one fully invested in the leadership of training the next generation of gospel preachers for the church. *Letters to My Students, Volume 2: On Pastoring* is a great compliment to the first volume as pastoring becomes the central focus and emphasis of this book. Dr. Allen lives what he teaches. He cares about pastors deeply, and I am certain this will be a helpful book for me as a current pastor and for those training to one day join this great calling. As pastors, we need mentoring. I am grateful to have access to one of the best through the words of this book."

Dean Inserra, lead pastor of
City Church in Tallahassee, Florida

"In a time when pastoring has come to mean all kinds of things that have little to do with the biblical vision for the office, the Church needs regular reminders of the irreducible complexity of biblical ministry. This is why I'm grateful for Jason Allen's latest volume in his *Letters to My Students* series. Volume 2, *On Pastoring* proves a reliable survey of a true shepherd's ministry both faithful and fruitful, and above all, oriented around the glory of Jesus."

Jared C. Wilson, assistant professor of pastoral ministry, Spurgeon College and director of the Pastoral Training Center, Liberty Baptist Church

"In this second volume of his *Letters to My Students. Volume 2: On Pastoring*, Dr. Jason Allen has provided a wonderful treatise for prospective, new, and seasoned pastors. Writing with a pastoral heart and from pastoral experience, Dr. Allen helps prospective pastoral students understand their call to ministry and prepare for what that call entails. He provides new pastors with an introductory manual for ministry—what every new pastor needs to know. And finally, he calls seasoned pastors to return to the basics. Whether you love God's people and want to shepherd them faithfully or love pastors and want to encourage them lovingly, you'll want to pick up this book."

Dr. Juan R Sanchez, senior pastor of High Pointe Baptist Church in Austin, Texas, and author of *The Leadership Formula: Develop the Next Generation of Leaders in the Church*

"Dr. Jason Allen is helping to change the world by investing his life in ministers of the gospel of Jesus Christ. By writing to his students, he pours his life into the next generation of Christian leaders. Blending his former service as a pastor with his personal scholarship as a seminary President, he brings a biblical and passionate vision for the church. This is why I hope you will read this book."

Dr. Ronnie W. Floyd, president/CEO of the Executive Committee of the Southern Baptist Convention and pastor emeritus of Cross Church

"Many pressures pull pastors in many directions. This book calls them to keep their eye on the ball: Here is your job description in the Bible, pastor. Don't forsake it. Jason Allen combines this call to Scripture with the wisdom earned through his own pastoral experience, giving readers a clear-eyed view of the wonderful work of pastoring."

Dr. Jonathan Leeman, editorial director at 9Marks and elder at Cheverly Baptist Church

"'The call to pastor is the highest calling known to man.' This quote from my friend, Dr. Jason Allen, sets the tone for his new book, *Letters to My Students, Volume 2: On Pastoring*. In this excellent work, Dr. Allen encourages and challenges local church pastors to willingly, prayerfully, and soberly embrace the daunting tasks that are involved in leading a local church. This work is filled with encouraging, practical information and challenges for every pastor. I highly recommend it."

Dr. Steve Gaines, senior pastor of Bellevue Baptist Church in Memphis, Tennessee

"In *Letters to My Students, Volume 2: On Pastoring*, Dr. Allen takes a fresh look at what it means to be a pastor in the twenty-first century. In this book, you will glean insights about the joys and the challenges of pastoral ministry: serving and preaching, feeding and leading, as well as, guarding and guiding the flock the Lord has called you to oversee. Whether you're a new pastor serving in your first pastorate or you've been pastoring for decades, you will learn biblical principles that apply to your current ministry context."

Dr. Robby Gallaty, senior pastor of Long Hollow Baptist Church and author of *Growing Up* and *Replicate*

LETTERS

— *TO MY* —

STUDENTS

VOLUME 2

ON PASTORING

JASON K. ALLEN

LETTERS

— TO MY —

STUDENTS

— VOLUME 2 —

ON PASTORING

B&H
PUBLISHING
NASHVILLE, TENNESSEE

Published by B&H Publishing Group
Nashville, Tennessee

Dewey Decimal Classification: 254
Subject Heading: PASTORAL THEOLOGY / CLERGY /
MINISTRY

Unless otherwise noted, all Scripture is taken from the New
American Standard Bible, copyright © 1960, 1962, 1963, 1968,
1971, 1972, 1973, 1975, 1977, 1995 by The Lockman Foundation.

Also used: New International Version®, NIV® Copyright
©1973, 1978, 1984, 2011 by Biblica, Inc.® Used by permission.
All rights reserved worldwide.

Also used: English Standard Version. ESV® Text Edition:
2016. Copyright © 2001 by Crossway Bibles,
a publishing ministry of Good News Publishers.

Cover design by Brian Bobel. Photography by Cole Gorman.
Cover typewriter keys © REDAV/shutterstock.

1 2 3 4 5 6 7 • 25 24 23 22 21

DEDICATION

With great affection, I dedicate this book to my boyhood pastor, Fred Wolfe. It was under Dr. Wolfe's preaching that, as a freshman in college, I came to faith in Christ. Even before coming to faith in Christ, in hindsight I see how blessed I was to grow up under his ministry. As a child I heard the inerrancy of Scripture preached, the lordship of Christ upheld, and the necessity of the new birth proclaimed.

Though Brother Fred's faith has now become sight, I remain indebted to him for his many decades of faithful ministry. The prophet Isaiah tells us "How beautiful are feet of those who bring good news of good things." As one to whom Dr. Wolfe brought the gospel message, his feet remain beautiful to me.

ACKNOWLEDGMENTS

As with any writing project, this book would not have come to completion without the sacrifice and support of many. I remain profoundly indebted to each one of them.

At the personal level, my life and ministry is enabled and enriched by the prayers and encouragement of my family. God has abundantly blessed me with my wife Karen and our children Anne-Marie, Caroline, William, Alden, and Elizabeth, who have surpassed my every hope and dream as to what they'd be and mean to me. To my favorite six people on the planet, thank you.

At the institutional level, my colleagues and office staff likewise are a valuable source of support and encouragement. Most especially, I'm thankful for Tyler Sykora, Dawn Philbrick, and Lauren Hanssen. These people are an absolute delight to serve with, and they go about their daily tasks with graciousness and competence. Thank you.

Furthermore, I'm thankful to the team at B&H Publishers, most especially Devin Maddox and Taylor Combs. Thank you, dear friends, for believing in this project and for working with me to bring it to fruition.

Last, and most of all, I'm indebted to my Lord and Savior, Jesus Christ. Like every other ministerial undertaking, none of this would be possible without His grace, calling and enabling. May this book, and all that I do, bring Him much glory.

CONTENTS

FOREWORD

As I write this in early 2021, pastors face more pressure and are navigating more challenges than at any point in my lifetime. Crises related to the pandemic have not only taken a toll emotionally, physically and financially on congregations and pastors, they have become divisive. Pastors are criticized for being too political or not political enough. They take shots for addressing racial issues too often and for not addressing them enough. And the list goes on.

That is why I believe Dr. Allen's book could not have been more well-timed. In moments of crisis and question, we are often tempted to work harder, do things faster and become more isolated. When that happens, the stresses of ministry start to take an even larger toll. Turning to a book like this helps recalibrate your thinking and remind you of the reasons you answered the call to pastor in the first place. It also gives you a step-by-step guide when you feel like you may be floundering and just need some handles to grab on to while you regroup and get your bearings.

Of course, no book can or should replace God's Word in our lives. Make Scripture and your daily conversations with God the lifeline that keeps you anchored spiritually and ministerially. This is the only place you can turn for true restoration for your soul. In times like these, it's tempting to turn to other places for relief, but only God's Word and His specific words for you can provide what you need to shepherd your congregation and bring the truth to them.

As a pastor, never forget that you live each day on a spiritual battlefield. The church will always be under fire, and you will always be a target. Satan wants to distract, discourage, and defeat you. If you wake up each day with the goal of having a peaceful, conflict-free ministry, you will be ground down with discouragement in no time. Prepare yourself, protect yourself with your spiritual armor, and don't pretend that spiritual warfare is not raging around you.

As you practice that discipline, you must also protect your marriage and family. The only thing worse than not giving your church and ministry enough time, attention, and focus is giving it too much—letting it dominate everything including your marriage and family life. I am grateful for mentors who encouraged me to make marriage and family a priority early on in my pastoring years. The pastorate will always demand more than you can give, and demands are loud and consistent. Until a crisis occurs, the needs of your wife and family most often won't be so overt. Focus on them now. Give them the time they need and deserve. You are called to them as well.

Always remember that you have the best job in the world. With all of the challenges it brings, there is nothing in the world like being a pastor. It is a wonderful calling and privilege to lead God's people and to proclaim His Word. I hope you will make this book one that you turn to often. It is filled with wisdom, experience, and great ideas. And I hope you will never cease to hold up God's Word and let it shine brightly in this world that has never been more in need.

Dr. Kevin Ezell
President
North American Mission Board

SERIES PREFACE

Good books are like good friends. Both bring with them words of instruction and counsel. They are companions on life's journey, providing insight and encouragement along the way.

For the Christian minister this is doubly true. To be a minister is to be a reader. You read books to know the Bible and to mature as a teacher of it. And, like a friend, God often brings a book into our lives at just the right time. That's exactly what God did for me.

In my earliest days of ministry, while still processing God's call and exploring what a life of ministry would entail, a friend gave me Charles Spurgeon's *Lectures to My Students*. Spurgeon walked into my life at precisely the right time. *Lectures to My Students* proved not only helpful but also transformative. I would come to learn that *Lectures to My Students*, and the man who authored it, had equipped and inspired generations of ministers like me. I was hooked.

Who Was Charles Spurgeon?

In the words of Carl F. H. Henry, Charles Spurgeon was "one of evangelical Christianity's immortals."[1] Henry so labeled Spurgeon due to the expansiveness of his ministry and its continued reverberation after his death.

Spurgeon was a phenom. He preached in the largest church in the Protestant world situated in the most powerful city in the world, London; yet his ministry stretched even farther, coursing through the expansive tentacles of the British Empire. He embodied all that is right about biblical ministry and all that the contemporary church must recover in the twenty-first century: biblical faithfulness, evangelistic fervor, self-sacrificial ministry, power in the pulpit, social awareness, and defense of the faith.

As a preacher Spurgeon pastored London's Metropolitan Tabernacle, where he ministered for nearly forty years to a congregation of some six thousand members. Spurgeon is commonly ranked, along with George Whitefield, as one of the two greatest preachers in the English language. In 1858, he preached to a crowd numbering 23,654 at London's Crystal Palace, and by the end of his ministry, he had preached to more than ten million people without the aid of modern technologies.

As an author Spurgeon wrote with an unstoppable pen. By the time of his death, he had published approximately 150 books. His sermons, which were edited weekly and distributed globally, sold more than fifty-six million copies in his lifetime. In Spurgeon's day they were translated into more than forty languages and now total more than sixty-two hefty volumes. Additionally, Spurgeon wrote for various magazines and journals, including his *Sword and Trowel.*

As a humanitarian Spurgeon hurled his might at the great social ills of his day. He founded two orphanages and a ministry for "fallen women," was an ardent abolitionist, started a pastors' college, and began a book distribution ministry for undersupplied pastors. Spurgeon launched clothes closets and soup kitchens for members and nonmembers of the Metropolitan Tabernacle. By the age of fifty, he had started no fewer than sixty-six social ministries, all of which were designed to meet both physical and spiritual needs.

As an apologist Spurgeon ardently defended his Baptist, evangelical, and reformed convictions. He attacked hyper-Calvinism and Arminianism, Campbellism, and Darwinism. Most especially, Spurgeon defended the person and work of Christ and the comprehensive inspiration and infallibility of Scripture. Spurgeon's apologetic efforts were most clearly witnessed through the prism of the Downgrade Controversy, where he challenged and ultimately withdrew from his own Baptist Union for their equivocation over these same issues.

As an evangelist Spurgeon relentlessly preached the gospel and consistently won sinners to Christ. He remains an unsurpassed model for clinging tightly to both the sovereignty of God and the responsibility of man in evangelism. In fact, one is hard-pressed to find any sermon Spurgeon ever preached that does not conclude with a presentation of the cross. By the end of his ministry, Spurgeon had baptized nearly fifteen thousand believers.

Spurgeon's ministry is still shrouded in a certain mystique. This is, in part, because he was a genius. But it is also due to his indefatigable ministerial work ethic, which prompted David Livingstone to ask of Spurgeon, "How do you manage to do two men's work in a single day?" Spurgeon, referencing the Holy Spirit, replied, "You have forgotten there are two of us."

Lectures to My Students

Central to Spurgeon's legacy is his classic work *Lectures to My Students*. This volume developed organically, as the natural outflow of Spurgeon's Friday interactions with his pastors' college students.

Since these men had spent the week in rigorous study, Spurgeon styled his Friday sessions as more informal. He dealt with the practical aspects of preaching and pastoral ministry. Over time the counsel Spurgeon gave in those sessions was recorded and compiled into book form. Thus, Spurgeon's *Lectures to My Students* is brimming with biblical and practical advice for the minister. He covers everything from the call to ministry to calling on church members. He swerves back and forth from the theological to the practical, from the convictional to the preferential, from the mundane to the spiritual.

In so doing, Spurgeon gave his students a near-comprehensive text on the full range of issues related to preaching and pastoral ministry. *Lectures to My Students* has proven to be a timeless work, benefitting most every minister who reads it.

Letters to My Students

Thus, this volume—and entire series—is written in the venerable tradition of Spurgeon's *Lectures to My Students*. I know how much he helped me, and I want similarly to help you.

I'm inquisitive by nature; and as a new minister, I was especially so. Thankfully, I had a couple of mentors who answered my queries and pointed me to others who could do the same.

I now find myself on the other end of such questions and conversations. As a seminary president, I teach classes on preaching, pastoral ministry, and leadership. On a near daily basis, I converse with pastors and students about these topics.

Herein are my best answers. Over the years I've kept up with my correspondence, some in the form of literal letters, others in emails, classroom lectures, phone conversations, or conference sermons and presentations. These answers have found their way into my class lectures, and still others have migrated all the way to my website, where I often write on preaching and pastoral ministry.

In my role as a seminary president, I'm giving my life to equipping those called by God for more faithful and effective ministry. While that preparation is essential, it doesn't end when one walks across the graduation stage. Growing in ministry is a lifelong pursuit, and growing as a preacher is to be the same. The book in your hand is intended to help you toward these ends.

Why I Admire Pastors

Theodore Roosevelt, the twenty-sixth president of the United States, was one of the greatest elected officials in our nation's history. He was also one of the greatest leaders the world has ever known. A tsunami of energy, Roosevelt never saw a mountain too tall to scale or a fight too threatening to join. He shook the nation, invented the modern presidency, and left a changed country in his wake.

In other words, there is a reason why his face, along with Washington, Jefferson, and Lincoln is chiseled on Mount Rushmore.

Roosevelt, reflecting on the burden of leadership and the willingness to risk all and attempt great things, famously observed,

> It is not the critic who counts; not the man who points out how the strong man stumbles, or where the doer of deeds could have done them better. The credit belongs

to the man who is actually in the arena, whose face is marred by dust and sweat and blood; who strives valiantly; who errs, who comes short again and again, because there is no effort without error and shortcoming; but who does actually strive to do the deeds; who knows great enthusiasms, the great devotions; who spends himself in a worthy cause; who at the best knows in the end the triumph of high achievement, and who at the worst, if he fails, at least fails while daring greatly, so that his place shall never be with those cold and timid souls who neither know victory nor defeat.[1]

Every time I read Roosevelt's quote my mind darts to the pastorate, and the fine work men of God do. The office of the pastorate is a high one, the work a noble one, and the men who faithfully undertake it are worthy of our admiration. Unless and until they give me reason to think otherwise, they have mine.

In our age of constant news, social media excesses, and the world's voyeuristic interest in pastors who have morally failed, it is easy to forget all that pastors do for the church. Sure, we have all heard of a pastor who has not acted admirably, but they are the exception, not the norm.

The fact that I have spent more than two decades serving local churches also informs my admiration. I have stood in the pastoral gap. I have lived in the trenches of local-church ministry. I know what it is like to crank out sermons, bury dear congregants, deal with difficult members, confront those in sin, and lead a struggling congregation. I have endured the lows; I have enjoyed the highs. Through it all, the romance of God's call to ministry has never left me.

What is more, I now daily interact with pastors as a seminary president. Many are on the front end of ministry, preparing for their first church and eager for the same. Just as frequently, though, I interact with well tenured men of God. I hear their stories. I sense their struggles. I have lived their life and walked in their shoes. Whether you are an upstart minister or a long-tenured pastor, my heart is with you.

Yet, my personal experience as a pastor and my daily interactions with pastors are not the ultimate reasons I admire such men of God. My admiration is first driven by deeper, more convictional issues—matters of calling, stewardship, and biblical qualifications and responsibilities. At the outset of this book, review just a few of these reasons with me.

First, pastors are called by God. Christ has given the church, in our age, "Evangelists, pastors, and teachers, for the equipping of the saints for the work of service, to the building up of the body of Christ" (Eph. 4:11–12).

One does not stroll into the ministry; one surrenders to it. Pastors have been set apart by God, called by His Spirit, and submitted their lives to Him. It requires obedience not only to enter the ministry, but to continue in it. Thus, I admire pastors for yielding their lives to God.

Second, pastors minister the Word. The pastor's one irreducible responsibility is to feed the sheep the Word of God. Paul stipulates the pastor "must be able to teach," and he charged Timothy to "give attention to the public reading of Scripture, to exhortation and teaching" and to "preach the Word" (1 Tim. 3:2; 4:13; 2 Tim. 4:2). The pastor who faithfully discharges this responsibility does more than feed the church the Word; he feeds me the Word. Every Christian needs a steady intake of God's Word, and a faithful pastor, who rightly divides the Word weekly, is worthy of high praise.

Third, pastors are held to a higher level of accountability. This accountability begins with the qualifications of the office, as outlined in 1 Timothy 3:1–7 and Titus 1:6–9. But it extends to other passages as well, including "Let not many of you become teachers, my brethren, knowing that as such we will incur a stricter judgment," and that congregations should "obey their leaders and submit to them, for they keep watch over your souls as those who will give an account" (James 3:1; Heb. 13:17). This fact is all the more daunting when you realize that pastors face more intense temptation. Satan targets those whose fall will do most damage to the church and most sully God's glory. I admire pastors for putting themselves in the arena.

Fourth, pastors tend the flock of God. Pastors preach, lead, and fulfill a host of other ministerial responsibilities, but pastors also bear the burdens of their people. When we need prayer, counsel, or support, pastors stand in the gap for us. Paul spoke of his affection and parental care of the believers in Thessalonica, and Peter exhorted the elders to shepherd the flock with eagerness, not lording it over them. Such is the heart of a pastor, one who loves his congregation. This is no easy task. Church members can be wayward, stubborn, and even rebellious. Thus, the pastor who serves the flock is worthy of our admiration.

In Conclusion

Do you admire pastors? I sure do. If you are in or pursuing pastoral ministry, know that I admire you. In fact, most every pastor I know garners my trust and respect and deserves my prayers and support.

It is that spirit that motivated this book, and it is that spirit I hope you will detect as your read it. Pastors and future pastors, I am for you. I believe in you. I admire you. This book is to encourage you in your ministry labors and to strengthen your hand as you go about them. May God bless you in the work.

Chapter 1

Set Apart by God
The Minister and His Calling

The call to pastor is the highest calling known to man. This high view of gospel ministry prompted Charles Spurgeon to famously reflect, "If God has called you to be his servant, never stoop to be a King of men." If you are reading this book, you have probably sensed that call. In fact, you most likely resonate with Spurgeon's lofty assessment of pastoral ministry.

The work of pastoral ministry is indeed grand—thus, you should undertake it with a profound sense of spiritual opportunity and stewardship. No doubt, that is one reason why you are reading this book: you want to be better equipped for a faithful, fruitful ministry.

In this chapter, and as we open this book, I want to briefly frame for you the call to pastoral ministry and, in particular, your personal call to ministry.[1] What are the major indicators of God's call, and how do these intersect with your personal life and ministry? This is important not only as you enter ministry but will also serve as ongoing accountability and guidance throughout your ministry. As an entry point, let us first clear up common misconceptions about the call to ministry.

Calling: A Misunderstood Concept

Among evangelical churches, the call to ministry is often misunderstood. Some view the call to ministry as an altogether personal, individual decision. If one believes themselves to be called to ministry, that settles it. What gives the church, or any other deliberative body, the right to question what God called me to do? If a person self-identifies as called to ministry, that is evidence enough, so the argument goes.

Others view God's call as an entirely mystical, subjective experience. They believe that to evaluate one's call to ministry in objective terms is altogether unspiritual. They shrug off biblical expectations for ministry, such as 1 Timothy 3:1–7 and Titus 1:6–9. They view God as too big, too dynamic to confine Himself to His written Word. If someone thinks the Spirit is leading them into ministry, one need not be held up by biblical or congregational expectations.

What is more, others view the call to ministry in human, professional terms. They view a seminary degree, or some other ministerial credential, as sufficient qualification for ministry service. Just like attorneys,

physicians, and other professionals are marked out by
their formal training, so are ministers to be. Earn a
degree or gain a license for ministry and then pursue
religious work accordingly. It is as simple as that.

Still others view the call to ministry as a one-time
experience, and the biblical qualifications for ministry
a one-time threshold to cross. They believe calling to
be a past-tense reality. Perhaps on the front-end of
ministry one needed a church's affirmation and to meet
biblical qualifications found in places like 1 Timothy
3:1–7, but now it is a settled matter. Additionally, so
goes the argument, God leads you into ministry as a
life calling but is indifferent to where and how you
serve throughout your life. In other words, you are
free to move and maneuver the ministerial ranks as you
desire, not as God leads.

Lastly, many evangelicals view the call to ministry
as something one does not pursue but reluctantly surrenders to undertake. In fact, the common phrase "surrender to ministry" suggests as much. Yes, God initiates
the call to ministry, not man. Moreover, in a sense, the
spiritual office is to seek the man and not *vice versa*. But
the apostle Paul makes clear that "If any man *aspires* to
the office of overseer, it is a fine work he *desires* to do"
(1 Tim. 3:1, emphasis added). Note the words, *aspire* and
desire. It is not only appropriate, but necessary, for one
entering ministry to desire the work of ministry!

Clarity Out of Confusion

As a college student wrestling with the call to ministry, I was confused. It all seemed imperceptibly mystical and mysterious to me. I thought I sensed God's call to ministry but was unsure of precisely what I was to be looking for. I desired to serve in ministry but thought that desire inappropriate, perhaps a sign of pride or unhealthy ambition.

In God's kind providence a friend pointed me to 1 Timothy 3:1–7 and Charles Spurgeon's *Lectures to My Students*. Reading Spurgeon's book, especially his section on the call to ministry, and meditating on 1 Timothy 3:1–7 were of enormous help, giving me a breakthrough of clarity and certainty.

Paul's words to Timothy (and similarly to Titus, in Titus 1:6–9) framed my call to ministry then—and still do. Read and reflect carefully on this passage.

> It is a trustworthy statement: if any man aspires to the office of overseer, it is a fine work he desires to do. An overseer, then, must be above reproach, the husband of one wife, temperate, prudent, respectable, hospitable, able to teach, not addicted to wine or pugnacious, but gentle, peaceable, free from the love of money. He must be one who manages his own household well, keeping his children under control

with all dignity (but if a man does not
know how to manage his own household,
how will he take care of the church of
God?), and not a new convert, so that he
will not become conceited and fall into
the condemnation incurred by the devil.
And he must have a good reputation with
those outside the church, so that he will
not fall into reproach and the snare of the
devil. (1 Tim. 3:1–7)

Additionally, Spurgeon's *Lectures to My Students* is
a timeless work on ministry service. In fact, I deliberately played off of Spurgeon's classic in the title of this
book series, *Letters to My Students*, as my own tribute
to Spurgeon, who is widely acclaimed as the prince of
preachers. Spurgeon helpfully unpacks signs of the call
to ministry, most especially the first sign as "an intense,
all absorbing desire for the work."[2] For me, this point
was clarifying and even liberating and compelling for
my life and my call to ministry. I learned God had
placed that desire in my heart. That assurance propelled
me forward, launching me to the next stage of reflection
and deliberation.

The Gravity of the Call to Ministry

As I continued to pursue ministry service, I increasingly sensed the gravity of that calling. Doing so did not dissuade me, but it did awaken me to the majesty of ministry service. I found myself resonating with Charles Bridges, who wrote on the gravity of ministry some 200 years ago. Consider his words with me:

> Who, whether man or angel, "is sufficient" to open "the wisdom of God in a mystery"—to speak what in its full extent is "unspeakable"—to make known that which "passeth knowledge"—to bear the fearful weight of the care of souls? Who hath skill and strength proportionate? Who has a mind and temper to direct and sustain so vast a work? If our Great Master had not himself answered these appalling questions by his promise—"My grace is sufficient for thee;" and if the experience of faith did not demonstrably prove, that "our sufficiency is of God;" who, with an enlightened apprehension, could enter upon such an awful service; or, if entered, continue in it?[3]

In order to find our balance here, we should review the apostle Paul's words to the Ephesian believers. He writes in Ephesians 4:11–15,

> And He gave some as apostles, and some as prophets, and some as evangelists, and some as pastors and teachers, for the equipping of the saints for the work of service, to the building up of the body of Christ; until we all attain to the unity of the faith, and of the knowledge of the Son of God, to a mature man, to the measure of the stature which belongs to the fullness of Christ. As a result, we are no longer to be children, tossed here and there by waves and carried about by every wind of doctrine, by the trickery of men, by craftiness in deceitful scheming; but speaking the truth in love, we are to grow up in all aspects into Him who is the head, even Christ.

In the context, Paul unpacks for us how God is building His church, and how essential pastors and teachers are to His plan. Furthermore, Paul shows how Christ equips His church and how the church is central to God's eternal purpose and redemptive plan.

Notice what Paul says in verse 11. He begins by unpacking specific offices Christ has established for the church. The first two, apostles and prophets, have long been understood to be first-century offices given for a season until the church was established and the canon of Scripture was closed.

But in verse 11, we see that Christ has given His church leaders today and for all times in the form of evangelists, pastors, and teachers. These leaders have been given their proper role and function by none other than Christ Himself.

If this calling by Christ is not weighty enough in and of itself, Paul goes on to state the reason Christ has given His church these leaders is "for the equipping of the saints for the work of service, to the building up of the body of Christ" (v. 12). This results in a church that is spiritually healthy, theologically sturdy, and missionally united. What a task. What a calling. What a stewardship we have!

Calling: A Checklist to Consider

All of this reminds us we must be sure about God's qualifications for ministry and certain He has set us apart for such service. Along these lines, review with me seven questions, indicators that God has called you into the ministry:

> 1. *Does your character match God's expectations?* First Timothy 3:1–7 and

Titus 1:6–9 are paramount here. You should carefully review and reflect on these passages. Moreover, you should invite others to assess your life along these lines and remember that these qualifications are not a one-time threshold to cross, but are an ongoing expectation for the minister.

2. *Do you desire the work of ministry?* As we have seen, longing for the work of ministry is not only appropriate; it is essential. That inner longing for ministry will serve as a magnet, pulling you forward throughout various seasons and trials of ministry. If ministry is one of many opportunities before you, each seeming similarly attractive, that is a sign that you may not be called to the ministry. As the apostle Paul makes clear, you should desire the work of ministry.

3. *Are you gifted to teach the Word?* As you review 1 Timothy 3, you will note the only real difference between the office of the deacon and the office of the elder is the ability to teach. Of course, there are varying levels of accomplishment. Gifting, training,

experience, and a host of other factors will determine how strong you are as a preacher and/or teacher, but the pastor must have a baseline ability to minister God's Word to God's people.

4. *Do you currently see fruit from your ministry activities?* By this, I mean: Have you seen God bless some of your efforts in the ministry so far? Have people seemed to benefit from your teaching and preaching? Have you been able to lead anyone to Christ? These are just a few questions that you can use to gauge the fruit of your labor. If you have not seen any fruit so far, that does not necessarily mean you should give up. Rather, go to your pastor and seek more opportunities, and pray fervently for God to bless your efforts.

5. *Are you passionate about the gospel and the Great Commission?* A passion for the gospel is a good sign that the Lord is calling you to ministry. As we shall see in the pages ahead, when Paul reflected in Romans 10 on the gospel, he was emphatic that people cannot hear the gospel message

without a messenger delivering it to them. If the idea of people coming to faith in Christ does not stir you, that is not a good sign.

6. *Does your church affirm your calling?* Ultimately, all the preceding questions are to be adjudicated by the local church. The Bible indicates the local church is responsible to call out the called. More specifically, the local church is responsible for who it calls to minister to the congregation. The church knows best how fit an individual in their midst is for ministry. Look to them for affirmation.

7. *Finally, are you willing to surrender?* As I wrote earlier, the idea of surrendering to ministry is often misunderstood, and I once misunderstood it. But, the one who would minister faithfully must be submissive to God's call whenever and wherever he issues it. That is not just as you enter ministry, it is throughout your ministry. Throughout your ministry, God will call you to specific tasks and to specific people, some more desirable than others. Will you follow wherever he leads?

In Conclusion

It is fitting to begin a book on pastoral ministry by clarifying and celebrating God's call to it. Even as I type these words, I am overjoyed by God's kind providence in my life, setting me apart for ministry service and strengthening me for that service over the years. I trust it does you as well. Let us now turn our attention to the work of pastoral ministry.

Chapter 2

Preach the Word

The Minister and His Pulpit

I t was February of 1998. I was a junior in college, had recently left my college basketball team to pursue ministry, and was trying to make sense of my life, my apparent calling, and what my future held. I was at a strategic crossroads, something like my own crisis of faith.

At this point, I had far more questions than answers. I sensed God's call to preach but was somewhat immobilized, trying to sort out what it meant—and what it would mean for me.

It was then I heard a friend say, "He's like the John MacArthur of the north." I quickly learned that the "he" was John Piper, who was slated to deliver preaching lectures in Birmingham, and my friend convinced me to make the drive with him.

In the days that followed, a (slightly damaged) car full of us loaded up and trekked north to Samford

University, where, to economize, we all crammed into one hotel room. Once there, we arrived early each day to hear Dr. Piper deliver Beeson Divinity School's Conger Lectures on Preaching. So early, in fact, we secured front-row seating for all of the sessions.

Hearing Dr. Piper's addresses proved pivotal for my life. Since then, our paths have not crossed much, but that week was something of a personal inflection point, and Piper's sermon on 2 Timothy 4:2 was key. It was a focusing moment, wherein I grew to appreciate preaching and link it—and the primacy of the pulpit—to the calling of pastoral ministry, for the two are inextricably intertwined.

Preaching: Priority 1

It is no coincidence that this chapter on preaching is situated just after the calling chapter in this book on pastoral ministry. To preach and teach the Word of God is the first priority, the central responsibility of the pastor.

As you likely know, in the preceding volume of this trilogy, I penned an entire book on preaching. For a fuller treatment on this topic, I point you there.[1] But in this chapter, and still in the foundational section of this book, I want to cover the big questions and the broad contours of preaching. Preaching is just too essential for me to assume you have read volume 1—though I hope you have, or soon will.

For now, let me remind you how essential preaching is to the life and ministry of a pastor. Admittedly in the twenty-first century, pastors wear many hats and carry out many responsibilities. Preaching is his first priority, but not his only one. In fact, we will review many of these hats and responsibilities in the chapters that follow. But within the context of the local church, preaching is the pastor's preeminent role. It is what makes the preacher indispensable in the life of the local church. It has always been this way.

To preach means to herald, to lift up one's voice, to proclaim. It is to speak boldly, even loudly, without fear. It is to unapologetically make known the truth of God.

God sent forth the prophets of old to preach. The Gospels tell us both John the Baptist and Jesus came preaching. At Pentecost, the church was birthed through preaching. Throughout Acts, the preaching of the apostles upended the world and fertilized the church. The office of deacon was formed to facilitate prayer and the ministry of the Word. Paul customarily went to the synagogue and reasoned from the Scriptures.

As we come to the Pauline epistles, we are told in 1 Timothy 3:1–7 that the elder must be "able to teach." In 1 Timothy 4, Paul told Timothy he came to "give attention to the public reading of Scripture, to exhortation, and to preaching." And, of course, in 2 Timothy 4:2, Paul charged Timothy—and through Timothy, us—to "preach the word."

Church history teaches us this as well: the men who have most mightily advanced the church and shaken the world have done so through the pulpit. Peter preached. Paul preached. Augustine preached. Luther preached. Calvin preached. Knox preached. Edwards preached. Whitefield preached. Spurgeon preached.

As Protestants, our own church life reinforces this. Our architecture places the pulpit front and center. In as much as we have a liturgy, it features preaching as the central component. Our jargon reinforces this point (or at least once did): pastor search committees were once called "pulpit committees," a call to ministry was a "call to preach," and the pastor was often simply called "the preacher."

Paul's Last Words Are Lasting Words

Paul's final charge to Timothy to preach the Word carries a particular weight and enjoys a lasting endurance as a ministerial charge. And it should. In context, there is a certain heft to Paul's exhortation to Timothy. They are the dying words of a dying man to a distressed church and a discouraged son in the faith.

Paul knew his death was near and he knew that empire-wide persecution of Christians was underway. This had accelerated mass defections from the church. Apostasy and disavowal of the faith were too common.

Timothy himself was vacillating, equivocating, in need of strength and personal fortification.

Every man called to preach can easily read himself into 2 Timothy 4:2. It has a certain romance to it. It has a magnetic pull, calling us to it again and again. We easily identify with Timothy, we hear Paul's voice, as it were, we feel his concern, and we desire to heed his admonitions.

It is Paul's word to Timothy, to the church, and, in a real way, to us. The pastor is to be a preacher—he must preach the Word.

Together, let's frame up the broad contours of how a pastor faithfully preaches the Word. To do so, we will work from 2 Timothy 4:2, the passage in which Paul's charge to "preach the word" is situated.

Preach Textually

Standing front and center in these verses is Paul's charge to preach the Word. Often, pastors read the text more as "PREACH the Word." For our purposes—and I think more reflective of the spirit of the passage—we should read it as "preach the WORD."

In fact, the emphasis on the text of Scripture roars throughout this entire book, culminating in chapter 4. Note with me key passages such as:

- 2 Tim. 1:13—"retain the standard of sound words."
- 2 Tim. 2:15—"be diligent to present yourself approved to God as a workman who does not need to be ashamed, accurately handling the word of truth."
- 2 Tim. 2:25—"the Lord's servant is to gently correct those who oppose, hoping God to grant them repentance so they may come to the knowledge of the truth."
- 2 Tim. 3:10—"you followed my teaching."
- 2 Tim. 3:14—"continue in the things you have learned from me and become convinced of."
- 2 Tim. 4:3—"they will not endure sound doctrine."
- 2 Tim. 4:4—"will turn away their ears from the truth."
- 2 Tim. 4:7—"I have kept the faith."

In the middle of all of this, Paul makes the divine assertion that "all Scripture is inspired by God and is profitable for teaching, reproof, correcting, and training in righteousness, so that the man of God may be adequate, equipped for every good work" (2 Tim. 3:16–17). The doctrine of the verbal, plenary inspiration of Scripture comes directly from this text, and upon this foundation comes Paul's imperative to preach the Word in chapter 4.

Further, note the simplicity of Paul's command to preach the Word. There is no need to clarify which word or whose word. We are called to preach God's Word, *the* Word. The Bible is our message. It is our Word. It is a perennial, necessary Word.

Is there not an apparent, intriguing irony in this simple charge to preach the Word? There almost seems to be an odd imbalance between the tremendous neediness of the human heart and the prescribed solution. The spiritual reality is an inverted one: spiritual hardness, darkness, and death are combatted with a simple tool: the preached Word. It is a man and a scriptural message, a preacher and his Bible.

Preach Expositionally

Scripture's unambiguous assertion to preach Scripture is the central reason why I am committed to expository preaching. By expository preaching, I mean the call to interpret and explain the text, in its context, and to bring it to bear in the lives of the hearers.

Again, I wrote of this extensively in *Letters to My Students, Volume 1: On Preaching*, but briefly review with me here twelve reasons why we should be committed to biblical exposition:

1. Expository preaching most deliberately fulfills the biblical commands regarding preaching.
2. Expository preaching best honors authority and status of Scripture.
3. Expository preaching gives authority to the sermon.
4. Expository preaching gives appropriate seriousness to your pulpit ministry.
5. Expository preaching matures the congregation.
6. Expository preaching demonstrates for your church how to study the Bible.
7. Expository preaching ensures relevance in the pulpit.
8. Expository preaching most consistently presents Christ and a robust gospel message.
9. Expository preaching, and the study it requires, matures you as a man of God.
10. Expository preaching gives the pastor confidence in his sermon.
11. Expository preaching most optimally stewards the pastor's time in the study.
12. Expository preaching best ensures balance in the pulpit.

In summary, I am absolutely convinced that expository preaching best positions the pastor to most faithfully preach the text. Faithfully preaching the text should be every pastor's ambition; it should be every pastor's self-expectation.

But some people might not like it if we preach this way. Some people may even leave the church, you surmise. I do not say this casually, nor am I indifferent to local church dynamics. In fact, we want to strive to bring God's people along with us. We want to do our best to draw them in, not push them away. But, in the final analysis, let's worry less about responses to our ministry, and more about adequately obeying the thrust of God's Word as we fill the pulpit with His words. Let God worry about filling the pew.

Preach Authoritatively

The first rule of golf is, as you approach the ball, you play it where it lies, as it lies. Preaching demands the same of us as we approach the text. We preach the text where it lies, as it lies. We are not to round edges or to force it into compliance with our favorite points of systematic theology. Preach the text where it is, as it is.

This principle is especially true when it comes to the more pointed passages of Scripture. Sometimes our fear of man or modern sensitivities prompt us to want to soften the barbed texts, to flatten the point, to round the edges. That is not our prerogative. We are to preach the text, every text, and to preach it authoritatively.

We are to "be ready" in season and out. To be ready is to "standby, equipped, alert, poised and on hand." Of this phrase "be ready," John Stott notes, "Here it appears to take on the flavor not just of alertness and eagerness, but of insistence and urgency."[2]

What is more, Paul says we do so "in season and out." This means whether the audience is receptive or not, whether the timing of the sermon seems particularly opportune or not, and whether you feel up to it or not. In other words, whether or not the church is ready to receive it or you are ready to give it, you preach the Word with authority.

Look with me more closely at Paul's chosen words in this verse. To "reprove" is a negative, corrective word. It carries the idea of challenging errant thinking and false doctrine. To "rebuke" is a reference to the heart, bringing a person under conviction of sin. John MacArthur writes that to "reprove discloses the sinfulness of sin, whereas to rebuke discloses the sinfulness of the sinner."[3] And, to "exhort" means to come alongside of and encourage, to show the way and exhort others toward it.

In other words, preaching is to be more than a data dump. The central liability of many would-be expository sermons is just that. We are called to be more than rambling commentaries. We are to present the text with force, probing our listeners.

Here is a key point we dare not miss: there is a correlation between biblical conviction and biblical preaching.
It is hard to have a truly high view of Scripture without
a high view of biblical preaching, and it is hard to have a
high view of preaching without first having a high view
of Scripture. We must have confidence and conviction
not only about what the Bible is, but also about what we
are to do with it: preach it authoritatively.

Preach Pastorally

Second Timothy 4:2 concludes with Paul's clarifying
word that we are to carry out our bold, authoritative
proclamation with pastoral awareness and sensitivity.
He says to do so with "great patience and instruction."

In many ways, that is what the remainder of this
book is about. Therefore, we will not belabor the point
here. But we must remember, pastors, even as we preach,
that we are called to shepherd the sheep, not to drive the
herd. When the passages call forth a rebuke, we do so
with humility, not hubris. We bring the Word to bear
pastorally, not unnecessarily painfully.

It almost seems too lofty an ideal: to preach the text
with authority, yet also with pastoral care and sensitivity. But that is exactly the standard set before us in
2 Timothy 4:2. It is a noble standard because it is God's
standard, and it is a standard that we should strive to
achieve.

In Conclusion

Preaching is the pastor's first priority. Preparing to preach will occupy most of your time, and preaching will require much of your energy.

Pastor, treat preaching as seriously as you can, then treat it more so. To be called to pastor is to be called to preach. It is who God made you to be, it is what He has equipped you to do, it is how He has gifted you to minister. Embrace it. Rejoice in it. Relish it. For local church ministry all starts in the pulpit.

Chapter 3

Prepare the Sermon
The Minister and the Study

Though as a child I enjoyed a healthy local church experience, preparing sermons was altogether alien to me. I assumed it was largely a subjective, spiritual process. Over the course of about two years, I muddied my way through leading a few Bible studies, unsure of how to study the passage before me.

About this time, I started helping, on occasion, with a ministry to women recovering from substance abuse. On Sunday afternoons, I and a few other men from my church ministered the Word to these needy ladies. The ministry was raw but also rewarding.

One week the gentleman who coordinated this outreach asked me to bring the message for the following Sunday. I was both exhilarated and terrified, eager to deliver a sermon but altogether unsure of how to prepare one. As Sunday approached, I grew increasingly panicked. I had trouble settling on a topic (not knowing

I should go to a text first). I jotted down my testimony, my favorite Bible verses, a few sports illustrations, and all the preacher jargon I could recall.

As you can imagine, my sermon was an absolute train wreck. I ran through my scrambled notes in about twelve minutes, then rebooted them and ran through them again. If I had delivered the sermon in a homiletics class, I would have failed the course—and rightfully so.

My main problem was not a lack of effort. Rather, I was just lost! The entire sermon process, from preparation to delivery, was altogether mysterious to me. Not only did I not know where to go for Bible study resources and interpretive help; I did not even know such tools existed.

You can imagine my surprise and delight when I was asked, a few months later, to lead a Sunday school class. We were slated to study the book of Colossians, and my college-ministry director handed me several commentaries. I was blown away that such study helps existed. I immediately began to learn how helpful the right tools are and how essential time in the study truly is.

To Be a Pastor Is to Be a Student

To be a pastor is to be a lifelong student, continually studying God's Word to preach it more faithfully and to minister to God's people more effectively. This experience is not just for those who minister in the twenty-first century. Rather, gospel ministers throughout the ages have known the importance of careful interpretation and the rigors of sermon preparation.

In fact, Paul exhorted Timothy to "be diligent to present yourself approved to God as a workman who does not need to be ashamed, accurately handling the word of truth" (2 Tim. 2:15). If Timothy, who knew Greek, was taught the Hebrew Scriptures as a child, *and* who was discipled by Paul, needed to study, so do we.

What is more, while in prison, Paul requested Timothy to "bring the books, especially the parchments" (2 Tim. 4:13). The great apostle himself prioritized study—even while imprisoned!

Commenting on this, Charles Bridges writes,

> It is indeed a "neglect of the gift of God that is in us," to trifle either in the study or in the pulpit. God will bless our endeavors—not our idleness. Our Master, and our people for our Master's sake, have a just claim to our best time and talents, our most matured thoughts, and most careful studies. To venture upon this infinite work of God with slender furniture, proves a guilty unconcern to our high responsibility. Admitting that some gifted Ministers may preach effectively without study; yet reverence for

our Master's name, and a due consideration of the dignity and solemn business of the pulpit, might well serve to repress a rash and undigested exercise of this holy function. How unequal to the exigency is the gathering of a few abstract and unconnected truths, without weighing the most forcible modes of application to the consciences and varied circumstances of our people.[1]

Though Bridges's words are, perhaps, more sobering than you are used to, these are needed words in our current context of pastoral ministry. When some pastors are content to put in minimal effort in sermon preparation, we need a contrary voice calling pastors to do the hard work of study.

In saying this, don't forget that there should be a sense of delight when it comes to the study. Week in and week out, you get to take deep plunges into the depths of God's Word. It is truly incredible that God has called you to spend your life doing this!

As I often tell my students, to preach is to live in final exam week. As Sunday approaches, every pastor feels the urgency of the task at hand. The fleeting minutes to prepare fly by, and the awareness increases that you will present the fruits of your study before God and man. The sensation of urgency you felt during final exam week in college is a weekly way of life for those who pastor.

Why Give Yourself to Your Study?

Is this life-as-finals-week really worth it? Why should the pastor be so concerned with sermon preparation? In Acts 6:4,[2] the apostles themselves reminded the early church that prayer and the ministry of the Word are the most important duties of the pastor. Lest you think I am overstating the commitment, consider with me these seven reasons:

First, the character of Scripture. The nature of Scripture demands we work to know it, to interpret it rightly, and to preach it faithfully. After all, it is not our word, it is God's Word, and only it is sure, certain, and authoritative. The Bible is indeed divinely inspired, fully inerrant, and absolutely infallible. Moreover, it is authoritative for life and doctrine and sufficient for the church. Carelessness in the study undermines our stated commitment to the Scriptures. The Bible deserves our best effort—let us make sure we give it just that.

Second, the stewardship of your calling. Commensurate with the call of God to pastoral ministry is the gifting to teach the Word. In fact, that expectation is stated explicitly in 1 Timothy 3:2.[3] God does not require what He has not granted. When He called you to be a pastor, He gave you the gift of teaching. Sure, each pastor will have his own level of gifting and ability; however, each pastor should strive to consistently improve that gifting and ability. You can actively do this by giving yourself to the study.

Third, it is a prerequisite to preaching. As we have already observed, Paul states that those who do not rightly interpret the Word of truth heap shame upon themselves. We simply must not enter the pulpit or stand behind a lectern without suitable preparation. Perhaps the only thing worse than preaching unprepared would be preaching undressed. Let us love God's people enough to not subject them to either.

Fourth, the needs of the church. Most congregations are pathetically ill taught. Decade after decade, they have been subjected to shallow teaching and weak sermons. Furthermore, often a lack of discipline in their own lives leaves them doubly malnourished. Take it upon yourself to strengthen the church, biblically and theologically, while they are under your watch.

Fifth, our cultural moment necessitates well-pre-paredness. Our church members enter Sunday having been shaken by the events of the week. Social unrest, shifting morals, political chaos, ethical dilemmas, and a host of other confusing issues fill their minds. They need a certain, sure Word from Scripture to renew their minds. Work hard in the study so you can counteract through the Word a week's worth of nonsense from the world.

Sixth, for your own spiritual nourishment. Though our sermon preparation should not displace other Bible reading and meditation, it should nonetheless be a devotional exercise for us. Hours in the study deepen our love for God's Word and our knowledge of the same. The truth of the matter is, your congregation needs to be nourished by the fruits of your study, but you may need it even more than they do.

Seventh, for your own self-respect. Do not succumb to laziness in your study, staleness in your spiritual life, or shallowness in your sermons. If you do, it will have a deleterious effect on your congregation. And it will have a similar effect on you. You do not want to enter the pulpit without spiritual assurance and confidence in your knowledge of the text. If you do, it will rob your preaching of power and you of self-respect.

How to Optimize Your Sermon Preparation

For the remainder of this chapter, I want to walk you through fifteen brief words of application to strengthen your time in the study, specifically your sermon preparation. You can work with all your might, but if you are not working wisely, you will still end up in undesired places with the text and undesired outcomes with your sermons. Thus, consider with me these fifteen quick tips for sermon preparation:[4]

1. *Be prayerful.* Ask the Holy Spirit to aid you as you study God's Word. Ask Him to help you understand it and apply it. We believe in the perspicuity of Scripture (that it is clear and that you can know what it means), but that doctrine should not negate our dependence on the Holy Spirit; it should necessitate it. Additionally, not all texts are equally perspicuous. His Spirit will help give you clarity in your time of need.

2. *Be early.* Do not wait until the eleventh hour to begin preparing your sermon. That will most likely lead to disaster. Sure, men like Charles Spurgeon often waited until Saturday night to prepare Sunday's sermon. But he was a genius. Most likely, you are not. The sooner you come to terms with the text, the longer you will have for it to marinate within you. Start early.

3. *Be focused.* Nothing hinders your study like interruptions; avoid them at all cost. Silence notifications on your phone (or just turn it to airplane mode). Determine to stay off

social media. Pick a place and times that you'll not be easily accessible. Consider setting goals for your study, resolving not to "get up" for any reason until you accomplish what you set out to do.

4. *Be well-resourced.* When it comes to study tools and sermon helps, contemporary preachers have an embarrassment of riches at hand. A simple online search will produce more materials on most any text or topic than you have time to read. Ask trusted ministers of the Word for their recommended resources and invest in good books. Mark them up and return to them again and again. Good books are well worth the price paid.

5. *Be inquisitive.* Asking the right question can unlock a text for you. Be inquisitive. Bombard the text with the big six: who? what? why? when? where? how? Also, be aware that if you have lingering questions about the text, the congregation likely will too. Interrogate the passage and prepare scripturally based answers. Your job as the preacher is to clarify the

text in the minds of your hearers, not to leave them more confused than you found them.

6. *Be humble.* If your passage has you stumped, ask for help. Turn your attention to online resources. Email an old seminary professor. Call an older brother in the ministry. The worst thing to do is to draw unwarranted interpretive conclusions. There are always answers to be had. You have not suddenly come across a passage that no one in church history has adequately explained. Seek out help!

7. *Be careful with commentaries.* We have already reflected on how invaluable commentaries can be, but do your own exegetical work first. Over the years, and on average, I have consulted five to ten commentaries while preparing a sermon on any given text. But I have learned that if I go too early to a particular commentary (especially if it is by an author I find particularly helpful), it may prejudice my interpretive conclusions before doing my own study. So, in short, definitely

use commentaries, but be intentional about when you open them.

8. *Be textual.* Build your sermon on a text and determine to know the passage before you better than anyone else in the building. You may well have mature believers in your congregation who know the Bible, or parts of it, better than you do. That is fine. Over time, God will grow you. It is okay not to be the most accomplished biblical scholar in the room. You cannot control that. But you can control how well you know Sunday's passage. Immerse yourself in the text.

9. *Be accurate.* Begin with accuracy in your interpretation, but do not end there. Determine for your sermon, from start to finish, to be accurate. Make sure the tone, outline, and contours of your sermon all accurately reflect the text.

10. *Be overprepared.* You want to approach Sunday pruning your sermon, not frantically in search of filler. Determine to compile a warehouse of material, then refine it into a showroom of presentation. What is more, it is always better to

enter the pulpit with too much preparation than too little.

11. *Be confident.* If you are called of God, are living a pure life, and have given yourself to suitable preparation, you can enter the pulpit with confidence. And enter with confidence you should. Confidence is not something you talk yourself into five minutes before you preach. It is a certainty deep within you that God has called you, that His Word is indeed true and powerful, and that you are prepared to be used by Him. If these things are true of you, then you can be confident; indeed, you should be confident.

12. *Be authoritative.* Building upon the previous point, you are preaching the authoritative Word of God; you should preach it authoritatively! Do not be unnecessarily harsh, but do not be apologetic either. You are the Lord's prophet—act like it. As Paul told Timothy, "preach, reprove, rebuke, and exhort" (2 Tim. 4:2). You may not be doing your job if you do not occasionally offend your hearers. "The task of the preacher," as Vance Havner has

said, "is to comfort the afflicted and afflict the comfortable."[5]

13. *Be specific.* As the saying goes, a mist in the pulpit is a fog in the pew. Work hard to be as clear as possible. Avoid the passive tense. Remove the word "things." Replace the generic with the specific. Transition from the abstract to the concrete. Quote Scripture accurately, and convey the chapter and verse. Cite your quotations. In short, remove as much ambiguity as possible from your sermon.

14. *Be Christ-centered.* You should be intentional to point your people to Christ in your sermon. To do that you will need to draw lines from your text to Christ in your study. Ask yourself questions like, "Where does my passage fall within God's work in redemptive history?" Remember the dual authorship of Scripture. Ground ethical imperatives in the gospel of Christ.[6]

15. *Be content.* Once you have preached the sermon, rest well. You have done your job; now let the Lord do His. It is the Lord's work, not your own.

You can trust in Him. You can rest
in Him. You can rejoice in Him.
Purpose to do just that.

In Conclusion

I have always enjoyed time in my study and have
always found sermon preparation to be life-giving. But
I did not always get as much out of it as I should. As I
have read books on hermeneutics and homiletics, as I
have completed seminary degrees, as I have grown as
a student and preacher, and most of all, as I have been
mindful of study tips such as these fifteen, I have ben-
efited. I bet you will as well.

Chapter 4

Shepherd the Sheep

The Minister and His People, Part 1

Still getting situated into my first pastorate, I well recall my first encounter with a "crisis" pastoral visit. Though I had served as a staff member for several years and had been unexpectedly called out for ministry needs, this was different. I was now *the* pastor—the *new* pastor—and the urgency in the voice on the other end of the phone meant they wanted *me*, and they wanted me *now*.

The call could hardly have come at a worse time. My wife, Karen, and I were settling in for what we thought would be a quiet Saturday evening. We had recently brought our first child home from the hospital. My sermon preparation was complete, our baby was tucked away, sleeping soundly, and we were gearing up for a slice of Little Caesar's pizza and a rented movie. Big times, right?

But this one, unanticipated phone call upended our plans. What should we do? What should I do? As the new pastor, I instinctively thought I should err on the side of going. My supportive, accommodating wife encouraged the same. My new congregation seemed sweet and supportive. Our ministry there had started so positively. I did not want to abruptly end the honeymoon period because of my pastoral negligence.

I apologetically slipped out of the parsonage, promising my wife I would return as soon as possible. Every minister reading this book knows—or will soon know—scenarios just like this. What should you do?

In this chapter and the next we're going to work through the topic of "The Minister and His People." First, in this chapter, we'll dig into most every aspect of personal visits and engagement.

Shepherding the Sheep

Biblically speaking, the pastor is called to shepherd the sheep. Many of us more naturally lean into the "feed the sheep" responsibility to the neglect of shepherding the sheep. But that is not biblical. Yes, Paul commends a host of ministerial characteristics and duties, including preaching and teaching the Word, but he also instructs us that the pastor must be hospitable, not pugnacious, gentle, and peaceable (1 Tim. 3:3).

Moreover, to the church at Thessalonica, Paul reflected, "We proved to be gentle among you, as a nursing mother tenderly cares for her own children. Having so fond an affection for you, we were well-pleased to impart to you not only the gospel of God but also our own lives, because you had become very dear to us" (1 Thess. 2:8).

You cannot be all things to all people, nor can you go everywhere for everyone. God is omnipresent; you are not. But on balance, people are not a hindrance to your ministry. People *are* your ministry.

Let's think through pastoral visits and how best to handle them. To help us sort this out, let's consider the types of visits you encounter, categorize them accordingly, and develop a plan for each.

The Crisis Visit

Crisis visits arrive unannounced and with the expectation that you respond with urgency. Though it begins as someone else's crisis, if handled poorly, it might create a crisis for you as well. Crisis visits are typically physical (medical emergency or unexpected death) in nature, sometimes relational (marital conflict or a wayward child), and occasionally spiritual (a sin issue or assurance of salvation). Regardless of the specifics, it is now your problem to solve. What will you do?

When crisis visits arrive, the most important thing to do is to discern if it is *truly* a crisis. For instance, the story I opened this chapter with turned out *not* to actually be a crisis. I would soon learn this church member was an alarmist and would periodically call in a panic. When she, or a similar individual called, I would work to corroborate the facts and what, if anything, I should do about it.

To this end, I would typically call the chairman of the deacons. He was well respected, typically in the know, had long-standing relationships with most every church member, and was always supportive of me. A quick phone call to him would clarify the entire situation. This simple step of gathering whether or not it was a crisis has proven to cull out the majority of such "emergencies."

If, on the other hand, the crisis is real, do you need to be the one to respond? Perhaps a ministry staff member or a lay leader, based upon their personal relationship with the one in need, or some other reason, is the most appropriate person to respond. If that is the case, feel free to enlist help, especially if circumstances limit your personal availability.

If it is truly a crisis and you are the most appropriate person to respond, you should view it through the lens of God's providence—God wants you there. Similarly, if you are simply out-of-pocket (out-of-town or otherwise) but the circumstances merit your personal response, I would encourage you to help your congregants see it through the lens of God's providence: "I would have been there, but God had other plans." Enlist the help of someone else and then personally follow-up with a phone call.

Medical Visits

Whether in the home or hospital, there are a few principles to keep in mind on medical visits. On the front end, sense how serious the condition is. That will set the tone for your time together, and frame how much you need to engage and follow up with other family members. As has been said, if it is *your* surgery, there is no such thing as minor surgery. It is always major. The one you are visiting often is more concerned than the medical facts merit. Keep that in mind.

In general, you need not stay too long. Typically, twenty to twenty-five minutes is enough time to read Scripture, pray, interact a bit, and then tactfully slip out. They are probably tired, and they understand you are busy. You would rather depart with them thinking, *I wish he had stayed longer,* than *I wish he had left sooner.*

If you feel the need to wait until their health condition clarifies, bring work with you to do. You can slip out to a nearby location, work on a sermon or other responsibilities, and tell the family you will check back in later but to call you if anything changes. More delicately, if the patient appears to be near death, you will have to sense the family's desire for you to stick around. A tactful conversation with the attending physicians may be helpful.

I remind you, however, that knowing when someone will pass is an impossibility. Our days are numbered by the Lord and known only by Him. I once was scolded by a family member for leaving before his loved one passed. I perceived her death was not imminent, and the attending physician signaled the same. The elderly lady wound up living another two years. The truth of the matter is, you may well die before the "near-death" person does.

Bereavement Visits

Perhaps no visit is more sensitive than the bereavement visit. Death, when it comes, brings with it pain and grief, no matter the circumstances. Sure, the death of a ninety-year-old saint is different from the unexpected death of a child. But there is a finality to death that makes it hard, regardless of the specifics.

When you visit a family in the hours or days after a death, read Scripture, speak softly, pray, and follow up. Strive to make contact soon after the passing of the loved one. It will enable you to minster to the family most effectively and to help shepherd and shape the funeral service. Many families have never planned a funeral service before. You can bring comfort by helping with the logistics, and you can serve them by graciously rooting out bad ideas for the service.

You should also have a good sense on the front end if it is likely that you will be called upon to officiate the funeral. If you desire to officiate the service, it is appropriate to offer your services to the family. We will have more to say on this in our chapter on weddings and funerals.

Soul Care Visits

As a goal, over the years I have striven to visit with church members annually. When that is numerically unmanageable, I have enlisted other ministry staff or lay leaders to help. In these visits, which generally have been well-received, I talk through how the family members are doing spiritually, how I can pray for them, how they are involved in the ministries of the church, et cetera. By making it well-known that the church pursues such annual visits, pastors ensure families and individuals they are not being singled out.

However, there are times when someone is being singled out, and that is in the early stages of church discipline as outlined in Matthew 18. In this text Jesus gives us a four-step process for implementing church discipline. He states in Matthew 18:15–17:

"If your brother sins, go and show him his fault in private; if he listens to you, you have won your brother. But if he does not listen to you, take one or two more with you, so that by the mouth of two or three witnesses every fact may be confirmed. If he refuses to listen to them, tell it to the church; and if he refuses to listen even to the church, let him be to you as a Gentile and a tax collector."

Jesus' words are fairly straightforward, but they are rarely practiced in the church today. Regardless of the specifics, if someone is living in persistent sin, especially public sin, the church needs to graciously confront the individual. In these situations, it is often best to show up unannounced, or else they will intentionally avoid you. Make sure you are operating in concert with Matthew 18 and, if applicable, your church's covenant and bylaws.

In this category, I also want to touch on visits with home-bound church members. You should have some set rhythm for you and/or ministry teams to visit with these dear saints. Once a month is the stated goal of many churches. Again, you will need to sense congregational expectations on this front and enlist elders, deacons, or other appropriate individuals to help shoulder the load. These can become the sweetest visits you will have, especially if the one you are visiting was an active church member for many years.

Outreach Visits

Lastly, let's consider outreach visits. Broadly, these are people who have visited the church or gotten connected through some other circumstance. Regardless of how the connection began, you have the opportunity to share Christ with them. If they have visited the church or you have some prior point of connection with them, make an appointment. Depending on your context, it may still be appropriate to show up on someone's doorstep unannounced. Yet, increasingly that is considered off-putting and too forward.

In these visits, you are trying to tactfully clarify their spiritual state. Ask them questions like if they have a church home, when they became a Christian, how they became aware of your church, what their spiritual background is. Arrive equipped to tell them about the ministry of the church, and, of course, the gospel message itself.

Odds and Ends

As we wrap up this chapter, there are a few principles with which I want to leave you. They will guide you well and are applicable to most every visit, regardless of the context or circumstances.

First, never go alone. Bringing someone with you will accomplish two purposes. First, it protects you in the event of false accusation or, heaven forbid, physical harm that may come your way. Second, you can mentor a lay leader or younger minister as you go. Soon enough, he will be in a position to lead visits himself. If the circumstances are right, I have also delighted in taking one of my children with me over the years. The alone time with them, and the opportunity for them to minister, have been enjoyable for me and formative for them.

Second, look the part. Social norms change and ministerial expectations vary from region to region, but, as a general rule, over dress, do not under dress. Be well groomed, punctual, and put together. When you want access to the ICU, you should not have to convince the nurse you are a minister. Look like one. Moreover, in bereavement and other moments of crisis, your presence—and appearance—ought to be reassuring. Leave the hoodie and flip-flops at home. Grab a collared shirt and jacket. Do not look like a kid fresh out of the youth department. Look like a man who is there to lead, to serve, and to minister.

Third, err in going, especially the first year. Be careful on this point. You do not want to set a pace you cannot maintain. At the same time, if you develop a reputation—warranted or not—for not caring, it will be nearly impossible to change it. Factors like how often your predecessor(s) visited, generational expectations, and whether the church is established or recently planted will all shape the congregation's expectations. Be mindful of these things, and, in the early months, err in going until you learn the lay of the land.

Fourth, always pray. This point is straightforward enough, but in nearly twenty-five years of ministry, I am amazed at how often ministers fail to pray, and how much it means to the one in need when we do. As a general rule, I have sought to pray for the person before and after the visit and with the person during the visit. Always pray.

Fifth, register your attendance. If you make a visit, be sure to register your presence. If the hospital patient is out of the room for tests, leave a kind note on the bedside tray. Ask the nurses to tell the patient you stopped by. If the home-bound church member is not available, slide a note in the crevice of the door. If a church visitor is not home, leave information about the church along with a personal note on their doorknob.

Practically speaking, to go to the trouble of making a visit but not indicate you stopped by is like attending an 8:00 a.m. class but not answering when the roll is called. If you make the effort to go, get credit for it. More importantly, leaving a note encourages the one to whom you sought to minister. Leave the note, pray for them in their absence, and move on.

In Conclusion

If the purpose of the visit is to connect with a person, you will have to work to make that happen from a scheduling standpoint. In general, try to visit during the lunch hour or during the afternoon. As a general rule, giving your mornings to God, your afternoons to administration and meetings, and your evening to your family works well. Yet you will at times have to be out on a weekday evening, Saturday morning, or Sunday afternoon.

Remember, times have changed. The mid-twentieth-century model of the omnipresent pastor has (thankfully) passed, but to be with your people you will have to *be with* your people. Do not dread those visits, but be wise about how you handle them. As you are, you will gain credibility with the congregation, more faithfully minister to your people, and find yourself leading an increasingly healthy, spiritually mature church.

Let's now turn our attention to the nuances of congregational life. As we'll see, it all starts with the word *love*.

Chapter 5

Navigating Congregational Life
The Minister and His People, Part 2

E aster Sunday is the biggest day of the church's calen-
dar year, surpassing even Christmas. Church sanctu-
aries that normally sit half-empty surge to capacity
on Resurrection Sunday. In addition to large attendance,
the service always arrives with added energy and joy—
for Jesus is alive.

Though I had experienced Easter Sundays as a
Christian and a church staff member, I was looking forward to presiding over my first Resurrection Sunday as
a senior pastor. Settled into my first pastorate for just a
few months as Easter Sunday approached, I anticipated
the grand day but felt a bit overwhelmed by how many
additional services and activities my congregation had
annually scheduled for Easter.

As the anticipated day drew near, I overheard hallway
conversations and began to field questions and requests
about Easter activities. Like most congregations, my

church had developed a pattern of adding events, ministries, and programs without pruning similar undertakings that had run their course. I saw a logjam coming.

I still recall putting pen to paper, outlining all of the services I would have to lead, activities I would have to coordinate, and events I would have to attend. Though Easter was still a couple months out, I was already tired just thinking about it.

Here is the lineup we enjoyed (endured): Wednesday evening, regular prayer meeting and Bible study; Thursday evening, Maundy Thursday service; Friday evening, Good Friday Service; Saturday morning, Easter Egg Hunt; Saturday afternoon, first Easter Cantata service; Saturday evening, second Easter Cantata service; Sunday morning, sunrise service, followed by an all-church breakfast, then Sunday school, and, of course, the Easter worship service; Sunday evening, regular Sunday evening service.

Whew! Just recounting those details makes me tired. But of all the services and events, there was one that particularly stood out to me: the Easter sunrise service. I had never attended an Easter sunrise service before, so I had no personal reference point. Moreover, the age of my newborn baby, an already over-packed Easter schedule, and the fact that I always use Sunday morning for final sermon review made me particularly dread the sunrise service.

Alas, the hour came. I still recall my wife situating our six-month-old baby into the car, then us driving the few hundred yards to Dickerson Lake, where we would gather for the service. It was a misty, foggy morning. As our Toyota Avalon eked along the gravel road slowly through the fog, we could see a small gathering of mostly senior adults taking shape.

In total, the crowd numbered about thirty individuals—the same faithful core who attended most all the other Easter activities and services. I made my way through the brief service, hoping to honor the Lord and minister to God's people, but truth be told, my attitude was lacking. That morning I found myself *enduring* the sunrise service.

A funny thing happened, though, over the ensuing years. As the years passed, I quit dreading the sunrise service. In fact, I came to look forward to that service. Indeed, these days, I miss gathering with those sweet people early on Easter morning by Dickerson Lake.

What changed? In the years that followed, we simplified our Easter schedule some, but the weekend was still quite full. In hindsight, I have come to see what changed, and it is not a what, it is a who. It was me. I changed.

As I came to know and love God's people in my church, I came to love what they loved too—which in this case happened to be an Easter sunrise service.

By way of analogy, the same is true in our marriages. Over the years, my wife has developed an appreciation for Boston Celtics basketball and regimental ties, and I have come to appreciate baked desserts and long walks. We did not enter our marriage appreciating these things, but we grew in our love for one another, and thus we have grown to appreciate what the other appreciates.

The same is true with a pastor and his people. A faithful pastor does not just love preaching, leading, or the trappings of local church ministry. He also grows in his love for his people and finds himself appreciating what they appreciate. Things like sunrise services—and other congregational peculiarities—that mean a lot to the congregation often come to mean a lot to the pastor too. As for me, as I grew in my love for my congregation, I grew in my love for what they loved.

When one considers navigating the nuances of congregational life, the love a pastor has for his people, and *vice versa*, is the right place to start. When mutual love exists, a foundation is laid for broader congregational health. When it lacks, a host of problems tend to emerge.

Loving God's People

In the New Testament, we see a pattern of pastors not just serving God's people but also loving them. Pastors preach, lead, shepherd, and fulfill a host of other ministerial responsibilities. Our lives are often too full, and our to-do lists too daunting. If we're not careful, we can undertake these duties in a clinical manner, causing them to become rote.

It ought not be this way. We are called to love the church. In fact, there is a distinct pastoral ethos we find in the New Testament—the minister is to love the people of God and give himself to them. Consider with me a couple of New Testament passages and reflect on them carefully.

In 1 Peter 5:1–4 (NIV), we see this loving, sacrificial heart of the shepherd come through:

> To the elders among you, I appeal as a fellow elder and a witness of Christ's sufferings who also will share in the glory to be revealed: Be shepherds of God's flock that is under your care, watching over them—not because you must, but because you are willing, as God wants you to be; not pursuing dishonest gain, but eager to serve; not lording it over those entrusted to you, but being examples to the flock. And when the Chief Shepherd appears, you will receive the crown of glory that will never fade away.

Again, in 1 Thessalonians 2:1–12, Paul unpacks his love for the Thessalonian believers:

For you yourselves know, brethren, that our coming to you was not in vain, but after we had already suffered and been mistreated in Philippi, as you know, we had the boldness in our God to speak to you the gospel of God amid much opposition. But we proved to be gentle among you, as a nursing mother tenderly cares for her own children. Having so fond an affection for you, we were well-pleased to impart to you not only the gospel of God but also our own lives, because you had become very dear to us. For you recall, brethren, our labor and hardship, how working night and day so as not to be a burden to any of you, we proclaimed to you the gospel of God. You are witnesses, and so is God, how devoutly and uprightly and blamelessly we behaved toward you believers; just as you know how we were exhorting and encouraging and imploring each one of you as a father would his own children, so that you would walk in a manner worthy of the God who calls you into His own kingdom and glory.

Do you see the New Testament picture? There are many different facets we could focus on, but the overarching ethos of the minister in the above texts is that he is one who gives himself fully to his people for their edification and good, all for Christ's glory. He should strive not merely to tolerate God's people, but to love them. In other words, people aren't a hindrance to your ministry—people *are* your ministry.

To love God's people as we should, we'll often have to deny ourselves and make undesired sacrifices on behalf of the church. The pastor has many imperfections, and a lack of love for his people may be one of them, but we should not settle for this. Instead, let's strive to cultivate our love for them and theirs for us.

Letting God's People Love You

It is a strange coincidence, but you will find that the more you let the church love you, the more they will. Some see danger in such intimacy. The theory goes that the more you let church members into your life and the more they see the "real you," the more likely they are to turn against you and to use that knowledge to harm you. To be sure, that has happened and may well happen to you. Yet, too often pastors set themselves up for relational breakdowns by never being relational in the first place.

On balance, letting the church love you will endear you to them. They will be more likely to know your personal needs, appreciate your desires for the church, and trust you as you lead them forward. As my colleague and friend Jared Wilson likes to say, "Our clothes should smell like sheep."

To be sure, intentional boundaries are important, and you and your spouse need to be mindful of unhealthy church members. Overall, though, opening your lives up to your church, and letting the members love you, is a win for them and for yourself.

Love Them, Warts and All

As I just acknowledged, the truth of the matter is, some of God's people are more lovable than others. The time you spend with some of your church members will be life-giving. You look forward to hearing from them. When their number appears on your caller ID, you light up. You look forward to an invitation to their house for a meal. You hope they will invite your family to a holiday gathering with theirs.

There are other members for whom that is just not the case. They are natural "Debbie Downers." You dread to see their number on your caller ID. When they poke their head in your office, you wince inside. You naturally want to avoid extended time with them. Whether it is because they are complainers, emotionally needy, or

just unenjoyable, every encounter with them is a draining one.

The gospel is for broken, needy people. Thus, we
ought not be surprised they are among God's people.
What is more, even spiritually healthy people do not
always have winsome personalities. You cannot spend all
of your time with the people in your church with whom
you most naturally connect. What should you do?

I encourage you to be intentional about ministry
time versus social or personal time. Of course, these
are not tidy distinctions, but over the years my pastoral
rhythm went something like this: I tried to honor all
of God's people and be ministerially available to meet
needs regardless of how much I naturally enjoyed being
with an individual or their family. Yet, I tried to make
my family's personal time and social outings enjoyable.
Thus, in those moments, we gravitated toward people
who were uplifting and encouraging and with whom we
had a more natural affinity.

Even pastors are not impervious to draining people.
We have to monitor the relationships in our lives and the
effects they have on us and our family. Strive to know
yourself, your family, and your needs, and your church
members and theirs. Intentionally allocate your time and
relational energy accordingly.

Protect Your Children

When we reflect on protecting our children, we tend to want to protect them from unhealthy church members. It is true: we should have an antenna for such people and be intentional to keep our children clear of them. But there is a more subtle, significant protection we must keep in mind—protecting our children from ourselves.

More than a few pastors' kids have been ruined by the pastor himself. Over time, your criticism will likely become their criticism; your negativity, their negativity; your cynicism, their cynicism. You best steward your children's hearts by protecting your own. You best steward their outlook by safeguarding your own.

To this end, my wife and I made a simple decision early in our ministry—never to speak ill of our church, or its members, in front of our children. We have adopted the same principle in our institutional settings and with our broader Southern Baptist family over the years. We want our children to age loving the church and the people who comprise it. There were times, especially when our children were younger, when some of their favorite church members were among the more difficult ones for me, but by God's grace, they never knew.

We are not in denial, and there are times when we have to unpack a particular ministry disappointment, congregational conflict, or problematic personality for our children. When we do, we must be careful in how we frame the issues and, in particular, the words we choose. Our children are perceptive. If you think it is time to engage them in such a conversation, it is probably past time. They probably picked up on the issue long ago. Here we trust the Lord's kind providence and our faithful shepherding of their hearts to carry the day.

However, such major issues are not my primary concern. Rather, I am most concerned about the throwaway line of sarcasm and the biting word of criticism. We all have fleshly moments when our frustration comes through, but if you give your children a steady diet of such, do not be surprised if they grow up resenting the church.

A Few Final Words

To pull all of this together, consider six final thoughts concerning how to effectively navigate congregational life:

1. *Establish healthy first-year precedents.* The patterns you establish in the first year of ministry will have a lasting impact on you and your place of service. If from the start you demonstrate a commitment to the study, an intentionality with pastoral care, and a devotion to your family, your members will likely see, appreciate, and respect those priorities.

2. *Know your capital.* Even for pastors and churches, relationships are like checking accounts. You only have so much leadership credibility (and thus capital) in your account that you can spend. You *accrue* capital as you lead wisely, preach faithfully, and shepherd diligently. Like compounding interest, longevity tends to increase your capital. You *spend* capital by confronting sin, preaching difficult texts, making hard decisions, and taking firm stands. You *lose* capital by flubbing sermons, dropping leadership balls, and needlessly alienating people. Work hard to accrue capital. Be intentional about how and when you spend capital. Try not to lose capital.

3. *Maximize your tools.* There's no presence like real presence, but in the absence of personal contact, a phone call, text, email, or even handwritten note goes a long way. Moreover, you might leverage social media to increase your pastoral communication and reach. In general, there is an inverse correlation between the efficiency of your communication and the power of its impact. By this I mean, the more time you spend, the greater the touch. A personal visit is more meaningful than a phone call, which is more meaningful than a note, and so forth. But these also require more time. If you are trying to simply pass along a word of update, a text will do. If you are trying to touch a heart, plan to meet in person.

4. *Remember the most strategic hour in your week.* You may well be able to accomplish more in a few

minutes before and after your worship services than you can in a few hours during the week. Being visible and accessible during these strategic moments will impact your church and save you more time than you can imagine. A strategic word to an irritated member might prevent a difficult elder meeting later that week. A quick word of prayer with someone facing a health crisis might well make unnecessary a subsequent hospital visit. A quick word of counsel and a strategic loaning of a book on marriage might well save you recurring counseling sessions—and their marriage. My point is not to try and find ways to skirt your pastoral duties. Rather, my point is that there is almost always too much to do in the week, so you should try and capitalize on your time and opportunities.

5. *Know your congregation.* Most congregations are dynamic, not static. Annually, a fair amount of people come and go. As studies have noted over the years, the composition of your church impacts their natural inclination to follow your leadership and support your ministry. As a general rule, those who join under your ministry and are your age or younger are typically most eager to support you. Those who precede you and are significantly older may take a little longer to develop their confidence in you. This should by no means discourage you, but you should keep it in mind as you seek to build some of that relational capital that I mentioned above.

6. *People need to like you.* By this, I am not suggesting you become a people pleaser, a "yes man," or that you choose to water down your preaching to avoid difficult issues. Rather, I am suggesting you work to be gracious, thoughtful, and appropriately endearing. You can be the best leader on the planet, but if your church does not like you, they will not be inclined to follow you. Likewise, you can be the best preacher on the planet, but if your church does not, in the main, like you, soon you will find yourself without a congregation to which you can preach.

In Conclusion

Every congregation, like every minister, is different. Your age, gifting, experience, convictions, stage of life, and a host of other factors shape who you are as a pastor and leader. Similarly, geographical context, congregational demographics, previous ministers, and much more shape the identity and outlook of the church. Do your best to sort out these distinctions in the interview process and determine all the more to do so once your ministry to them begins. Your calling and ministry are too consequential to be tripped up over mundanities.

Chapter 6

Raising Up Leaders in Your Church

The Minister and His Team

The French statesman Charles de Gaulle famously quipped that "graveyards are full of indispensable men."[1] De Gaulle was right. In the affairs of men, none of us are truly indispensable. This is true in the church as well. Pastors come and go, but the church marches on.

Realizing this principle early in your ministry will humble you, embolden you to build a supporting cast, and incline you to hand off ministry responsibilities to those around you. Investing a lot of time in a group of leaders in your church might at first seem counterintuitive, but for your long-term well-being (and for the church's) it is key. In ministry, the quality of your co-laborers is essential; therefore, the amount of time and energy you invest in them can often make all the difference.

Few things will influence the effectiveness of your ministry more than the ministry team with which you surround yourself. Some you will inherit; some will find you; some you will find. Regardless of the specifics, you must cultivate a leadership team who shares your convictions, your calling, and in whom you can place your confidence. Your ministry will come to depend, in large measure, on such a team.

Two Offices: Pastors and Deacons

In Scripture we find two offices for the church: pastors and deacons. In the New Testament, the terms for pastor, elder, and bishop are used interchangeably referring to one office.

For example, in Acts 20:17 Paul called the "elders" of the church at Ephesus. Then, addressing those very elders a few verses later in 20:28 he says, "Be on guard for yourselves and for all the flock, among which the Holy Spirit has made you *overseers*, to *shepherd* the church of God which He purchased with His own blood" (emphasis added). So, in this one context, there are three words (elder, overseer, and shepherd/pastor) used for the same people/office. Commenting on this passage, F. F. Bruce writes,

> There was in apostolic times no distinction between elders (presbyters) and

bishops such as we find from the second century onwards: the leaders of the
Ephesian church are indiscriminately
described as elders, bishops, (i.e., super-
intendents) and shepherds (or pastors).[2]

Most Baptist churches prefer the nomenclature of
pastor, though the moniker "elder" is becoming more
common. As to pastors, we ought not limit this to the
"senior pastor" position. It is for all who are ministering
the Word to the congregation in a formal, ministerial
way and who meet the qualifications of 1 Timothy 3:1–7.

In 1 Timothy 3:1–13, the qualifications for pastors
and deacons are remarkably similar. In verses 1–7, Paul
lays out the qualifications for pastors:

It is a trustworthy statement: if any man
aspires to the office of overseer, it is a fine
work he desires to do. An overseer, then,
must be above reproach, the husband of
one wife, temperate, prudent, respectable,
hospitable, able to teach, not addicted to
wine or pugnacious, but gentle, peaceable,
free from the love of money. He must be
one who manages his own household
well, keeping his children under control
with all dignity (but if a man does not
know how to manage his own household,
how will he take care of the church of

God?), and not a new convert, so that he will not become conceited and fall into the condemnation incurred by the devil. And he must have a good reputation with those outside the church, so that he will not fall into reproach and the snare of the devil.

Then, he follows with the qualifications for deacons in verses 8–13:

Deacons likewise must be men of dignity, not double-tongued, or addicted to much wine or fond of sordid gain, but holding to the mystery of the faith with a clear conscience. These men must also first be tested; then let them serve as deacons if they are beyond reproach. Women must likewise be dignified, not malicious gossips, but temperate, faithful in all things. Deacons must be husbands of only one wife, and good managers of their children and their own households. For those who have served well as deacons obtain for themselves a high standing and great confidence in the faith that is in Christ Jesus.

Essentially, the character and life-style expectations are the same, but the pastor must also be able to teach the

Word of God. Thus, as you look to build out a ministry team, whether lay or vocational, start with 1 Timothy 3:1–13 and work out from there.

Cultivating Lay Leaders in Your Church

Over time, your church will rise no higher than the leaders who serve it. Intuiting this principle during my first pastorate led me on a quest to find and nurture more faithful lay leaders. To this end, for years I led a Saturday morning men's Bible study. I selected twelve men who were leaders (or had the potential to be) and led them through select scriptural studies.

My criteria for participation were simple. I looked for men who already demonstrated leadership potential, but perhaps had been untapped. They were regular in worship, engaged in the life of the church, and seemed ready for more responsibility. Some of the invitees were long-time members, others were relatively new.

Given the time of the study (Saturday mornings) and the nature of the topics, the group self-culled with only the more serious men signing up and sticking with it. We spent months studying topics like biblical hermeneutics, the doctrine of the church, and systematic theology. When leadership opportunities developed, this group was a natural place to look. Deacons, Sunday school teachers, and AWANA leaders all came from this group.

The moral of the story is: do not be surprised if your church lacks leadership when you arrive. Most churches do. But it is not your job to complain about it; it is your job to change it. Invest yourself in key men and then be gratified when they invest themselves in the life of the church.

A vast majority of churches will not be in a position to hire additional staff. Cultivating lay leaders will be like lifeblood for the church—and for you.

Hiring Ministry Staff

If you are looking for a new staff member, and fortunate to be in a church that has the means to do so, making the right hire is key. A bad staff hire is—at minimum—a three-year mistake. It typically takes a year to become convinced it is not working out, a year to transition them out, and a year to get over their time with you. Moreover, you will likely burn a lot of personal capital through all the drama. In short, when a staff member fails, no one wins—including you.

When hiring a staff member, you should always be looking for the big three: character, competence, and compatibility. Does his life measure up to 1 Timothy 3:1–7? Does he have the necessary gifting for the ministry he will oversee to flourish? Is he a good fit culturally with you, the rest of the ministry team, and the church as a whole? To ferret out these issues, you will want to probe seven areas.

First, doctrinal alignment. Is he on the same page theologically with the church? Is he mature and settled, not trying to find himself theologically? For example, if he is still working through what he believes about baptism, it is best that he does not serve a Baptist church. Moreover, you will have difficulty emphasizing the importance of sound doctrine to your church if you do not underscore it in your ministry hires.

Second, personal piety. Over time, the church will reflect its leadership. While this is especially true for the lead pastor, it is also true for the broader ministry team and lay leadership. If the church's leadership is carnal or shallow, over time that will show up in the pew. Conversely, if the leadership pursues personal holiness, that too will be reflected in the congregation. To this end, inquire about his walk with God. Ask to hear his testimony of faith in Christ (and his spouse's). Inquire about his devotional life. Note not just what he says, but also his comfortability with the conversation in general.

Third, mission buy-in. Does he just want a ministry job or does he want to minister to your church specifically? Ministry is a calling. Not just in a general sense, but also to specific places of service. Sense if he has a heart for the people who will be under his watch. Probe to find out if he resonates with your church's mission statement and ministry initiatives. You want a team who believes in your work and does not need constant pep talks.

Fourth, ministry ambition. This is a careful point. We dare not confuse worldly ambition with ministry ambition. You want to avoid hiring a ladder climber, one who will serve only until a better opportunity comes along. At the same time, you want to avoid persons who are lazy, passive, or just trying to find themselves. You want to hire someone who is ambitious and energized for the church, the Great Commission, and serving the people of God.

Fifth, love of the flock. Sadly, some ministers love the idea of serving the church in the abstract, but do not particularly desire to serve the church before them. You will want to observe how he interacts with people, how he speaks of former places of service, and how he reflects on the ministry opportunity before him. If you hire from within the church, you will already know how the staff member relates to the congregation.

Sixth, cheerfulness and collegiality. Here we refer to the compatibility component. Can you envision him happily fitting in with the congregation? How about the rest of the ministry team? In general, can he identify with the church and can the church identify with him? You should not overthink this point, nor should you try to overly script it. God calls different people from different backgrounds with different personalities to serve in different contexts. But do make sure the gap is not so wide that it undermines one's ministry or sets one on a course for conflict.

Seventh, more than a job. Look for individuals who see the opportunity as a calling, not just a job. The latter will focus on job requirements, vacation days, salary package, and the technical, formal expectations of the position. The former will be mindful of the same but will focus on the ministry opportunity before him and how he can give himself to the church. To this end, observe how involved his family signals they intend to be, his willingness to help beyond the formal job description, and, in general, his heart for the ministry.

Odds and Ends on Staff Hiring

Look internal first, then external, being particularly mindful of previous places of service. Look for gaps in their résumé. Do not email references; call them. References will convey more verbally than in writing. Call every reference he gives you and some he does not. Remember, anyone can have a bad church experience, so do not disqualify a candidate for that. But, if he has racked up a number of them, beware. If he speaks ill of former pastors or churches, doubly so.

Always spend time with his spouse and children, if he has them. Do not judge them, but do observe them. Remember, people put their best foot forward in the interview. If you sense a problem then, it will likely get worse with time. Proceed with caution.

The process of hiring a staff minister will vary from church to church. You may have an elder board, personnel committee, or some other lay group with which you must work. Over the years, I have desired as pastor to give leadership to the search. Not only have I been happy to work with the appropriate laypersons, I have insisted on lay involvement too. There is wisdom in a multitude of counselors. A pastor who unilaterally hires and fires will likely, over time, get himself out on a limb.

Volunteer Staff

You may find yourself in a church large enough to necessitate additional ministry help, but not financially strong enough to pay for it. This is ministerial no-man's land, and many, if not most, churches are there. I have been there too.

Over the years, one way I have overcome this is by creating a ministry position with defined responsibilities but filling it with a volunteer until such a time when the church can pay that individual or hire someone else to fill it.

This has several upsides. First, as the church sees that more ministry can be done through a volunteer in the slot, it may prompt them to think bigger, conclude the position is essential, and find the money to hire someone. What is more, the act of creating the position will remind the church what ministry is not being done and why an additional minister may be needed.

The volunteer position can help the individual in it as well. I once pastored in proximity to a seminary (Southern Seminary in Louisville). I have had young men in my church who were faithfully doing the work of ministry. They were called, gifted, and committed, devoting much of their time to the church. By creating these volunteer staff positions, they gained valuable, formal ministry experience. Thus, they were better positioned to find full-time service upon graduating from seminary. It was truly a win for all parties: for the individual, for me, and for the church.

In Conclusion

Just as Aaron and Hur held up Moses' arms, so too will ministry partners hold you up. They are essential to your ministry effectiveness and longevity. You simply cannot do it all, and, over time, burnout or discouragement means that you will not. Timothy Witmer helpfully said,

> We look at a plethora of reports that come out year after year about pastoral burnout and the alarming number of clergy leaving their churches or leaving the ministry

altogether. Might not one of the contributing factors be that they are not receiving the help they need in shepherding the flock prescribed in the Scriptures? Not only will our churches be healthier, but the work of the pastor will also be more manageable if all elders take seriously the work that Christ has called them to do in sharing the responsibility to shepherd the flock.[3]

Always be on the lookout for ministry help, within your church and beyond. When you find the right people, enlist them, equip them, and empower them. As you do, you will benefit, as will the church.

Chapter 7

Membership Matters

The Minister and Church Membership

For a new pastor, few challenges are as vexing as inheriting a bloated membership roll. On the one hand, you feel the weight of giving an account for the souls entrusted to you (Heb. 13:17), but, on the other hand, you know that pruning your membership roll may well lead to churchwide conflict.

As a Southern Baptist, I find this challenge is particularly acute in my denomination. Roughly speaking, we have about 15,000,000 members on the rolls of about 45,000 churches. Yet, on any given Sunday only about a third of those show up to worship with God's people. Indeed, America's largest Protestant denomination has a membership problem. As Adrian Rogers once famously observed, "We Southern Baptists may be many, but we're not much."

Many factors have created this dilemma. Well-intended but sloppy evangelistic practices over the years have prematurely added names to rolls. Evangelicalism's emphasis on having a personal relationship with Christ has also subtly and unintentionally deemphasized church involvement—many who may nominally be members of a church are not active in any meaningful way.

Many Christians view themselves as free agents, rotating churches based upon which one "meets their current needs." Complicating matters is an over correction against Roman Catholicism. It is true that church membership does not save someone, but it does not follow that it's unimportant.

In recent years, ministries like 9Marks[1] have awakened many to the importance of meaningful church membership. Many pastors are feeling their way through this knotty issue, attempting to shepherd their congregations toward greater health. But is it worth the time, energy, leadership capital, and potential conflict it may bring?

In order to answer this question, we will survey the following: where we see church membership in the Bible, what we mean by meaningful church membership, why congregationalism demands meaningful church membership, and why meaningful church membership is important. We will conclude with a few words of practical advice.

Where Do We See Church Membership in the Bible?

One of the most common statements about church membership is that the words "church membership" are not found in the Bible. Does that mean that the concept of church membership is foreign to the Scriptures? No. Rather, though the words themselves are absent, the concept of church membership is implied all throughout the New Testament. Let's look at a few examples among many.

First, Hebrews 13:17 states, "Obey your leaders and submit to them, for they are keeping watch over your souls, as those who will have to give an account." From this text, we see that pastors will be held responsible for those whom they pastor. This implies that the pastors will know who exactly they will be held accountable for, that they will be able to differentiate between their members and nonmembers.

Second, Paul writes in 1 Corinthians 5:9–13 (ESV):

> I wrote to you in my letter not to associate with sexually immoral people—not at all meaning the sexually immoral of this world, or the greedy and swindlers, or idolaters, since then you would need to go out of the world. But now I am writing to you not to associate with anyone who bears the name of brother if he is guilty of

sexual immorality or greed, or is an idola-
ter, reviler, drunkard, or swindler—not
even to eat with such a one. For what have
I to do with judging outsiders? Is it not
those inside the church whom you are to
judge? God judges those outside. "Purge
the evil person from among you."

In this passage we see that there is an "inside" and
an "outside" of the church. The church is only to hold
accountable those who bear the name "brother"—that is,
those who are Christians. This text only makes sense if
the church is clearly demarcated by church membership.

Third, in Acts 2:37–47, we see that there is a numeri-
cal record of those who have been converted and added
to the church. Luke writes, "So those who had received
his word were baptized; and there were added that day
about three thousand souls." Clearly, the early church
kept a record of those who were added to the body.

While more passages could be considered, these
three give sufficient evidence that church membership is
clearly understood in the New Testament as imperative
for the Christian.

What Is Meaningful Church Membership?

The *sine qua non* of meaningful church membership is that your *members are regenerate*. Historically,

Baptists have referred to this as "regenerate church membership." This simply means that the individuals on your roll profess and give evidence of having a personal relationship with Jesus Christ. Collectively, your membership roll reflects men and women (and boys and girls) who are following Christ. That roll is dynamic, not static, as new members join and as, unfortunately, those who prove to not be true followers of Christ are removed.

Meaningful church membership necessitates *members who are baptized.* Lest you think this is a distinctly "Baptist" commitment, I remind you that in the history of the church, baptism (sprinkling or immersion) has been a prerequisite for membership and participation in the ordinances. Of course, as a Baptist, I am convinced the only legitimate baptism is post conversion, by immersion.

Meaningful church membership implies *members are active* in the life of the church. At minimum, this includes regularly attending worship and regularly giving. Depending upon the needs and opportunities of the church—and your personal life stage and circumstances—some form of service is typically expected as well. As to the particulars, the church should have a covenant or at least an expressed expectation of members. In other words, a member joins to participate, not occasionally observe.

Lastly, meaningful church membership includes *members who pursue holiness.* Historically, Baptists referred to this as a "disciplined church." Put simply it means that your affiliation with the church is not a liability to the church. The member lives in such a way that indicates he is a believer, and thus community members are not surprised when they learn he is a church member.

Why Congregationalism Demands Meaningful Church Membership

Before covering exactly why congregationalism demands meaningful church membership, it is first necessary to establish that the Bible actually teaches congregationalism. The first place we must look for the concept of congregationalism in the Bible is Matthew 18:15–20. But prior to looking at this text, we need to be familiar with what Jesus said two chapters before. Right after Peter confessed Jesus to be the Christ, Jesus said to Peter in Matthew 16:18–19 (ESV):

> "And I tell you, you are Peter, and on this rock I will build my church, and the gates of hell shall not prevail against it. I will give you [singular] the keys of the kingdom of heaven, and whatever you [sg.] bind on earth shall be bound in heaven,

and whatever you [sg.] loose on earth
shall be loosed in heaven."

At first reading, the singular "you" in this verse
appears to be giving Peter (and maybe the apostles if
Peter is their representative) outright authority to bind
and loose on the earth. It is no wonder the Catholic
Church uses this verse to support the papacy. However,
just two chapters later, Jesus helps us to understand what
exactly He meant in chapter 16. He says to His disciples
in Matthew 18:15–20 (ESV):

> "If your brother sins against you, go and
> tell him his fault, between you and him
> alone. If he listens to you, you have gained
> your brother. But if he does not listen,
> take one or two others along with you,
> that every charge may be established by
> the evidence of two or three witnesses. If
> he refuses to listen to them, tell it to the
> church. And if he refuses to listen even to
> the church, let him be to you as a Gentile
> and a tax collector. Truly, I say to you,
> whatever you [plural] bind on earth shall
> be bound in heaven, and whatever you [pl.]
> loose on earth shall be loosed in heaven.
> Again I say to you, if two of you [pl.] agree
> on earth about anything they ask, it will
> be done for them by my Father in heaven.

For where two or three are gathered in my
name, there am I among them."

Here, Jesus is walking His disciples through the
concept of church discipline. Notice that the same language from chapter 16 occurs here—that of binding and
loosing. Except this time, notice that it is in the plural,
"whatever you bind" or "whatever you loose." So, after
someone confronts a brother in sin by himself, he is to
take one or two more along, and then, if the person is
still unrepentant, it is to be reported to the church.

Next, and pay close attention here, *the assembly renders the final verdict*. The church is the one to declare
him "as a Gentile and a tax collector." It isn't the elders
or a presbytery or a bishop that makes the final call;
rather, it is the local church as a whole. As Jonathan
Leeman says, "With these two verses [vv. 17–18], Jesus
authorizes the entire assembly to wield the keys of the
kingdom."[2] Therefore, the church possesses the authority to bind and loose. Hence, in Matthew 18:15–20, we
see congregationalism very clearly.

Now, we will consider additional texts that point
to congregationalism, but these will not be considered
in as much detail as Matthew 18. In Acts 6, when the
church was experiencing incredible growth and when the
Hellenistic widows were being neglected, the apostles
summoned "the full number of the disciples," i.e., the
whole church, in order for them to "pick out from among

you seven men of good repute" (v. 3 ESV). While there is not space to argue whether this was the beginning of the biblical office of deacon, it is clear that the appointment of these men was the decision of the church, and not the apostles or elders.

In 1 Corinthians 5, when a man was living in detestable sin, Paul does not disfellowship the man himself or call the elders to do it, but rather, he calls the whole congregation to excommunicate the man. Commenting on this, Leeman states,

> What's fascinating about the episode is that Paul has made a judgment of his own and gives that judgment the full backing of his apostolic office, possibly invoking the name of Jesus Christ and the Spirit of God. And yet he still treats the Corinthian congregation like a younger brother who needs to be led, or discipled, but who must finally make the judgment for himself.[3]

Second Corinthians 2:6 possibly speaks about this same situation when Paul writes, "For such a one, this punishment by the majority is enough" (ESV). Whether this was the man from 1 Corinthians 5 is impossible to tell, but the significant point is that the punishment is by the majority, not by the elders or any other official church office.

From these passages, it is clear that the congregation has the final human authority in the churches. Congregational church governance means the ultimate, final human authority—and thus responsibility of the church—is the congregation. With such a weighty stewardship comes the necessity for the voting members to be regenerate, godly, and active participants in the life of the church.

Why Is Meaningful Church Membership Important?

First, it's biblical. Conventional wisdom suggests church membership is extrabiblical, a man-made construct by which pastors pigeonhole would-be church members. But, as we have seen above, that is simply not the case. Something not stated above that is important to keep in mind is that virtually every New Testament epistle is written to an implied readership—those within the church.

Second, the church is the repository of God's glory. On the earth, the local church is a kingdom colony, a kingdom outpost. The relative health and purity of the church bears testimony to the community. The community ought to see a difference in the lives and convictions of church members. Bloated membership rolls obscure God's glory in this regard. We reflect, for better or worse, God's glory.

Third, New Testament Christianity is congregational. In the New Testament, to be saved is to be in the church, and to be baptized is to be baptized into the same. You immediately enter a covenant community. In Scripture, there are no free-agent Christians roaming around. What is more, nearly every scriptural reference to the church is to a local congregation, as opposed to the church universal.

Fourth, we are Jesus' bride. Not to strain the metaphor, but the church is precious to Jesus. Jesus came for the church; He promised to build the church; He died for the church, is interceding for the church, and shall return for the church. We want the church fit, healthy, active, and, shall we say, beautiful for Him upon His return. Jesus deserves a compelling, attractive bride.

Fifth, the New Testament metaphors for the church imply collectivity. Think with me on this point. The Bible refers to the church metaphorically as a building, a body, a flock, a temple, and a family. Did you see the common feature? These are all comprised of groupings, of gatherings, of togetherness. What is more, the logic of the spiritual gifts is the same—God's people together, growing, serving, and edifying one another collectively. Christianity is a corporate endeavor.

Sixth, in the church, the sum is greater than its parts. When the church is together, one plus one equals three. Collective worship, collective ministry, and collective witness all surpass the effectiveness of spiritual lone rangers. Every Sunday my family leaves corporate worship encouraged by the congregational singing and fellowship with God's people. Congregational gatherings indeed have a stimulative impact, spurring the gathered church onward to good deeds and service.

Seventh, church membership brings spiritual accountability. This is true both for the people and for the pastor. There are legitimate reasons to miss church—even sometimes with regularity. Circumstances like illness, military deployments, family emergencies, occasional work responsibilities, and other providential impairments may be legitimate reasons to miss. Meaningful church membership positions the pastor to sort these things out, not just to wonder who is not in attendance and why. It also gives him and the body the tools needed to lovingly pursue wandering sheep.

A Few Words of Practical Advice

When being interviewed by the church, you should raise this topic as one you would like to see addressed. You can do it in a winsome, pastoral way, but you should inquire about the entirety of church membership. Ask questions like, "What is the composition of the roll? Has it ever been reviewed? How does one become a member? Is there a church covenant? How is it used in the life of the church? Do you have a new-members class?" You can communicate that you would like to see greater health in this area and that it is the pastorally sensitive thing to do.

As you embark upon cleaning up your membership roll, go slow. The church did not get there overnight, nor will it quickly get to a healthier position. Begin by informing and educating your leadership and the congregation as a whole why church membership matters. You should signal your desire to reach out and recover those members who have gone dormant, not abruptly cut them off. Again, be patient on this front. Moving in the right direction is a good step, even if the pace is slower than you desire.

As you begin to review your roll, you will find a host of reasons for the bloated membership. You may well have dead people on your roll, folks who have long since joined another church, or those who've relocated to another city. For those who are still on your roll and could (and should) be active, begin by communicating with them pastorally. Reengage them as the pastor.

As it becomes clear they have no intent to reenter the life of the church, perhaps create a negative trigger, so that by not responding they will, in effect, remove themselves from the roll. Keep their contact information for future ministry opportunities, but view them as they are, not as you wish they were. Treat them as prospects, not members. And remember, by their nonattendance and unresponsiveness, they have left the church, not *vice versa*.

Essential to this entire process is instituting a new members class. The shape of the new member process will vary from church to church, but it's clear you signal on the front end what it means to be a church member. The tragic reality is it is often harder to join a social club than it is a local church. Let that not be the case on your watch. The goal is not difficulty, but thoroughness. And you should want that. Remember, you will give an account for their souls.

Lastly, guard your motives. The goal is to shepherd the flock of God with care, leading your members and your congregation to greater spiritual health. The goal is not to boast to ministry friends about how many church members you pruned from your roles. Your ambition should be to recover, not to displace. To win them back (or over) to Christ, not to never hear from them again.

In Conclusion

As one who has served in local church ministry for more than two decades, I get it. The work to get one's membership in order is a daunting one. The path in that direction can be treacherous. Nonetheless, the church and its health are worth our best effort.

Move prayerfully and deliberately in this direction—but move. As you do, resolve to cultivate over the long haul a church that most reflects God's glory and a congregation that you are increasingly comfortable giving an account for.

Chapter 8

Administer the Ordinances

The Minister and the Lord's Supper and Baptism

One of the best parts of being a pastor is getting to lead your church in the observance of the ordinances. Of all the things Christ commanded His church to do, the ordinances hold a primary place. As a gathered church, we not only get to hear the gospel in the preached Word, but we also get to see the gospel through the ordinances. As you learn and grow as a shepherd, never forget the special place of the ordinances in the life of the church.

As a Baptist, I hold to two ordinances: the Lord's Supper and believer's baptism. The Roman Catholic Church, for example, observes seven sacraments: baptism (sprinkling), confirmation, the Eucharist, penance (for spiritual healing), anointing of the sick (for physical healing), Holy Orders (setting apart a priest, for example), and marriage.

Observant Roman Catholics believe the sacraments convey grace to the recipient *ex opere operato*—from the work worked. This is to say, the sacrament itself—not the condition, intent, or heart of the participant—is efficacious on its own to convey grace. As a Baptist, I obviously disagree.

Protestants understand there to be two ordinances for the believer: baptism, received once, and the Lord's Supper, received ongoingly. Thus, an ordinance is a practice instituted by Christ for His church to observe in perpetuity, until He returns.

More clearly, let's define an ordinance this way: a ceremony given to the church by Christ, practiced in the book of Acts, and expounded upon and defended in the Epistles. Two such practices meet these criteria—believer's baptism and the Lord's Supper. These criteria are why, say, foot washing is not a standing part of observing the Lord's Supper, and why baptism and the Lord's Supper are to be observed by the gathered congregation only, as opposed to household or small-group observance.[1]

Believer's Baptism

While I have been blessed by the writings of many who practice paedobaptism (infant baptism), I am very much committed to believer's baptism. This commitment is not based on my upbringing or other cultural factors. Rather, it is based upon an honest reading of the New Testament. I say this not to offend my paedobaptist friends (nor paedobaptists who are reading this book) but because I believe the case to be overwhelming.

A straightforward reading of the New Testament leads one to believer's baptism. I understand the arguments for infant baptism, but there simply is no scriptural reference or support for the practice.

As to what baptism actually is, *The Baptist Faith and Message 2000* defines it this way:

> Christian baptism is the immersion of a believer in water in the name of the Father, the Son, and the Holy Spirit. It is an act of obedience symbolizing the believer's faith in a crucified, buried, and risen Savior, the believer's death to sin, the burial of the old life, and the resurrection to walk in newness of life in Christ Jesus. It is a testimony to his faith in the final resurrection of the dead. Being a church ordinance, it is prerequisite to the privileges of church membership and to the Lord's Supper.[2]

In other words, baptism is both a symbol and a public act declaring our allegiance to King Jesus. It symbolizes our unity to the crucified and resurrected Savior, and it proclaims to the world that we have now aligned ourselves with Him and His church. Commenting on this second aspect of baptism, Bobby Jamieson has said well, "According to the New Testament, baptism is where faith goes public."[3]

Baptizing Children

As a pastor, one of the most ministerially challenging responsibilities you will have is whether or not to baptize young children who profess faith in Christ. As a convictional Baptist, it is hard for me to admit this, but when we baptize children too young to grasp the gospel and, as a result, whose hearts have not been affected by it, it is more troubling than sprinkling an infant.

Why is this? Because when Presbyterians, for example, sprinkle infants, they anticipate the child *will one day be converted*. When we baptize young children, we are testifying *they have been converted*.

To be clear, Jesus did not say children must become like adults to be saved. He said adults must become childlike. We are to encourage our children toward following Christ at every age, including the early years. However, if not careful, we can find ourselves routinely baptizing young children before they understand the gospel—or have been affected by it. Perhaps a subtle confusion over what conversion and baptism are lies at the heart of the matter.

As for conversion, we must remember it requires more than agreeing to facts about Jesus to be saved. Conversion is not merely intellectual; it is also affective. To be saved, one must not only embrace facts; one must embrace Christ. One must not merely believe facts about Jesus; one must believe in Jesus. This happens through faith in Christ, repentance from sin, and submission of one's life to Him. The point is not that a child cannot be converted; the point is that we should do our best to make sure conversion has happened in our children before baptizing them.

As for baptism, we do not believe in baptismal regeneration. Therefore, we should not rush one into the baptistery. Being baptized is a profound and essential step of obedience—one that is linked very closely with conversion—whereby one declares his or her allegiance to Christ, is baptized into the church, and depicts the death, burial, and resurrection of Christ.

For many reasons, including how closely conversion and baptism are linked in the book of Acts,[4] I am not for erecting age-based criteria, or adopting a programmatic, wait-and-see approach on baptizing new converts. Spurious conversions occur regardless of the age, and we are not called to wait them out before baptism.

Yet, a healthy understanding of conversion means we need not rush someone, especially children, to the baptistery. The effects of *true conversion* will not evaporate like the morning dew. When in doubt about whether a child is ready for baptism, it is best to give it time.

W. A. Criswell's practice helped me navigate this issue. During Criswell's half-century tenure at First Baptist Dallas, he encouraged young children—and older children who seemed not to grasp the gospel—to "continue to take steps toward Jesus," but often instructed their parents to hold off on baptism. He winsomely affirmed the child's interest in following Christ and encouraged them to that end, but he did so without granting them assurance of conversion or baptizing them straight away.

Criswell's pattern is instructive for every pastor. You can wholeheartedly press the accelerator on the gospel while tapping the brakes on the baptistery. That is not being duplicitous; it is shepherding the flock of God well.

As a pastor, I have joyfully baptized many children over the years. But I also have met with more than a few parents and encouraged them to hold off on pursuing their child's baptism.

For many pastors, especially those fearful of potential conflict, expressing reservations to parents about baptizing their child can be stressful. Yet over the years, I have had that conversation with parents many times. In all my years of ministry, I have never had a parent leave the conversation frustrated with me, or at least having expressed that frustration.

Generally, parents have valued my concern and appreciated my forthrightness with them. Moreover, since parents know I am willing to ask them to hold off, it has given them greater confidence—and joy—when, in due season, I have recommended baptism.

Many of God's mightiest men in church history experienced conversion at a young age. I do not question their conversion story—I thank God for it. Likewise, when a precocious young child understands the gospel, repents, embraces Christ, and reflects the fruits of conversion, we should celebrate that and baptize them as well. But if they lack any of these ingredients, caution and patience are key.

How to Baptize

Whether the candidate for baptism is a child or an adult, you should have them go through a baptism class. In so doing, you can sense their grasp of the gospel, teach them the meaning of baptism, and prepare them to share their testimony of faith in Christ.

On this latter point, I encourage you to have converts briefly share their testimony in the baptistery before you baptize them. How you handle this can vary from convert to convert. Some you may dialogue with, others you can simply let share for a couple of minutes.

As to the mechanics of baptism, I would encourage you to practice in the baptistery before you perform your first baptism in corporate worship. When it comes to what you might say during the baptism, there is no set formula. Consider the following as an example:

- Baptizer: "Do you repent of your sins and do you trust in Jesus alone for your salvation?"
- Candidate: "I do."
- Baptizer: "Will you continue to walk in faithfulness and obedience to the Lord Jesus Christ?"
- Candidate: "I will."
- *Begin baptism by holding their hand over their nose.*
- Baptizer: "Then I baptize you in the name of the Father, the Son, and the Holy Spirit."
- "Buried with Christ in baptism,"
- *Lowers into the water*
- "raised to walk in newness of life."
- *Raises from the water*
- *Baptismal candidate exits the water*

The Lord's Supper

Jesus instituted the Lord's Supper the night of His betrayal. As you will recall, He and the disciples entered the Upper Room and observed the Passover Feast together. In that setting, Jesus personalized it to Himself and pointed His disciples to this new observance that would eclipse the Passover Feast.

The Passover was the holiest of Jewish Feasts, commemorating their deliverance from the Death Angel and from Egypt into the Promised Land. Jesus transformed the Passover into a celebration of far greater importance—a deliverance from sin, an eternal deliverance, through the sacrifice of His own body and blood.

By the time we get to the book of Acts, it is clear that the Lord's Supper had taken root as an established practice. In fact, Acts 2:42 indicates the early church gave itself to the apostles' teaching, prayer, fellowship, and the breaking of bread (the Lord's Supper). Historically within Christendom, observing the Lord's Supper has been a consistent church practice, but what it represents and how to observe it, less so. Over the centuries, four views of the Lord's Supper have emerged. Let's briefly review these together.

Transubstantiation is the official belief of the Roman Catholic Church, adopted in 1215 at the Fourth Council of the Lateran. In the aftermath of the Protestant Reformation, in 1545 at the Council of Trent, the Roman Catholic Church reaffirmed transubstantiation. This view argues Jesus' words "this is my body" refers to His literal body and blood. During the celebration of the Eucharist, the Catholic Church teaches that the bread and wine become the literal body and blood of Christ.

Their view of the elements leads them to leave no consecrated wine (Jesus' blood) undrunk, and to lock away remaining consecrated bread (Jesus' body) in a box behind the chancel. When Roman Catholics enter the sanctuary, a suspended candle, if lit, signals the presence of Christ's body in the building. This prompts the entering one to genuflect.

Consubstantiation, as articulated by Martin Luther, is a step away from transubstantiation. Luther argued for the ubiquity of Christ during the Eucharist. Though the bread and wine are not Jesus' literal body and blood, He is, nonetheless, present in the elements and alongside the elements during the service. For Luther, *hoc est corpus meum* (this is my body) was inescapable. Though he rejected transubstantiation, his argument for consubstantiation is rooted in the same four words.

Real Presence, as expressed by John Calvin, is the third view. By Real Presence, Calvin argued Christ is truly present but only in a spiritual way during the Lord's Supper. Calvin's position proved to be a mediating one between Luther and Zwingli. Like Luther, the elements remind the church that Christ is present, as opposed to Zwingli who argued the elements remind us Christ is absent.

Memorialism, as advocated by Ulrich Zwingli, occupies the opposite pole of transubstantiation. Zwingli argued that Christ gave us the Lord's Supper—and in particular the physical elements of bread and wine—because

He is not with us on the earth. Thus, the elements remind us of His life, death, resurrection, and return.

Memorialism is the traditional Baptist view and is summarized in *The Baptist Faith & Message 2000* as "a symbolic act of obedience whereby members of the church, through partaking of the bread and the fruit of the vine, memorialize the death of the Redeemer and anticipate His second coming."

Observing the Lord's Supper

Having surveyed the common views on the Lord's Supper, let's now focus on actually observing it.

According to the apostle Paul, as outlined in 1 Corinthians 11:17–34, the Lord's Supper has five main purposes: *reflection* on Christ's sacrifice, *proclamation* of His atoning work, *examination* of our hearts, *celebration* of the forgiveness of our sin, and *unification* in bringing the church together. Each purpose is essential and should mark each observance of the Lord's Supper.

Some churches lean too heavily toward somberness in the Lord's Supper. In fact, it feels similar to an actual funeral service. You would think Jesus is still in the tomb and we were there to mourn Him! But this is not the spirit of New Testament observance. Reflection? Yes. Confession? Certainly. But the result is to be a celebration of what Christ has accomplished for us.

As to the question of who may observe the Lord's Supper, Christians have historically maintained that one must be baptized to come to the Lord's table. In that Baptists do not recognize sprinkling, Baptists have historically held that one must be baptized by immersion before participating in the Lord's Supper. This, too, is espoused in *The Baptist Faith and Message 2000* and is commonly referred to as "close communion."

On both ends of the "close communion" position are open and closed communion. Open communion invites all believers to participate in the Lord's Supper, regardless of baptism or church affiliation, and with inconsistent, if any, counsel on reflection and confession.

Conversely, closed communion maintains the Lord's Supper is to be only for a particular church. Thus, even if one is otherwise qualified to come to the Lord's Table, one is precluded if one is not a member of *that* church.

As to frequency of observance, practices vary from weekly to annually. Most Baptist churches observe the Lord's Supper quarterly. I encourage you to consider a monthly observance. Weekly observances almost necessitate the Lord's Supper be "tacked on" to the service. Quarterly or less frequently keeps the Lord's Supper on the periphery of church life. Observing the Lord's Supper ten to twelve times per year enables the church to focus on Christ's sacrifice with consistency while giving it due attention in the worship service.

In Conclusion

As a pastor, presiding over the Lord's Supper and baptizing new believers have been among my most cherished responsibilities. I pray they will be for you too. In the midst of the busyness of ministry, it can be tempting to allow the ordinances to take a back seat or to allow them to become rote and monotonous. I want to encourage you to recognize the significance of the ordinances in the life of the church. Teach your congregation their true significance. Ignorance often leads to ambivalence; therefore, teach your people to appreciate them. As you do, you and your people will be reminded of just how sweet Christ was to give us a picture of the good news we so love and cherish.

Chapter 9

Lead Worship

The Minister and Corporate Worship

I type this chapter in the midst of the Covid-19 crisis, which has necessitated that churches suspend corporate worship services for the foreseeable future. For months, churches where I live in Kansas City and across the country have not met together in person on the Lord's Day.

Even Easter Sunday, the most triumphant Lord's Day of all, had to be celebrated within the confines of our own homes. How long we will continue in this scattered state is unknowable, but it has left us longing to gather once more. Why? Because corporate worship is the divinely established norm for God's people. We were intended to gather in worship.

Covid-19, in a sense, has been a gift, because it has stirred within many of us a heightened desire to gather as the church. It has also prompted many pastors and churches to reflect anew on why corporate worship is so important, what it should comprise, and how best to lead God's people in it.

These are good and appropriate deliberations for all, but especially for the pastor. After all, he is the worship leader and his leadership on Sunday morning matters more than his leadership at any other time.

The Pastor as Worship Leader

Make no mistake, the pastor is the accountable party for the gathered worship. He may have a gifted worship minister, engaged elders, and a first-class tech support team, but the pastor must give leadership to the worship service. Coordinate with his ministry team, absolutely; altogether outsource the responsibility to others, never.

I want to be clear: Sunday morning is the one hour a week the pastor must get right. For many church members, that is the singular touchpoint with their church any given week. It is also the pastor's most strategic, and often only, weekly opportunity to feed the entire flock.

The pastor may on occasion forget an appointment during the week, let his email in-box overfill, or even wing a weekday Bible study. But he cannot flub corporate worship. For the pastor, every Sunday is Super Bowl Sunday. The pastor must lead with intentionality and deliberately construct worship services that honor the Lord and His Word. The question, therefore, is "What are the essential marks of a worship service?"

The Four Biblical Marks of Corporate Worship

While on vacation a number of years ago, I visited a church for Sunday worship but left questioning whether I had worshiped at all. I took in the full complement of announcements, shook hands with several greeters, viewed a skit, and enjoyed something of a concert. Though a rote prayer was offered, there was no congregational singing, Scripture reading, or a sermon. I left puzzled, frustrated, and with a sense of loss. I felt like I had visited a restaurant but was not served a meal. Nick Needham rightly describes the church I visited and others like it:

> The congregation has become an audience, the minister has become an orator, and everything else in the service can be safely ignored or even treated with casual contempt. Liturgy, creed, Scripture lections, confession, intercessory prayers, psalms and hymns, Eucharist—all have either been dropped or emptied of existential engagement. The only thing that matters is to be uplifted through the sermon. Subjectivity has won its first victory.[1]

What should a church do during its time of corporate worship? Or, perhaps better asked, why do churches do what they do during worship? These questions are necessary enough, but ask them in the typical church and they will elicit puzzled looks and confused answers.

What a church is to practice during corporate worship is not a new consideration. In fact, it was a pressing concern in Reformation Europe, and its answer continues to shape the twenty-first-century church.

The Regulative Principle Considered

The ordering of worship for Protestant churches has followed two general patterns over the past five centuries. Martin Luther advocated what became known as the *normative principle*, arguing the mass—as celebrated by the Roman Catholic Church—could basically remain intact, sans the aspects of Catholic worship that clearly violated Scripture. Gregg Allison says that the normative principle "holds that unless Scripture explicitly or implicitly prohibits them, other worship elements may be incorporated and the church's liturgy is still pleasing to God."[2] The Pandora's box-like openness of the normative principle is its most obvious and vexing liability.

The *regulative principle*, advocated by John Calvin and the Reformed tradition, argued the church should essentially start over, only permitting into corporate worship that which the New Testament explicitly calls for. Over time, the regulative principle became common practice in much of the Free Church tradition, including Baptist churches.

Based upon what is specifically prescribed in the New Testament, the regulative principle includes four features in public worship: Scripture reading; corporate prayer; singing psalms, hymns, and spiritual songs; and the preaching of God's Word.

Historically, *the public reading of Scripture* is seen as mandated in 1 Timothy 4:13, which states, "Until I come, give attention to the public reading of Scripture, to exhortation and teaching." Often, this passage has served as a scriptural call to worship—a reminder the church has gathered to hear from God. Often the congregation stands as it is read, showing reverence, deference, submission, and a physical reminder that the Bible is the Word of God.

Prescribed in Ephesians 5:19[3] and Colossians 3:16,[4] *singing psalms, hymns, and spiritual songs* has always marked the worship of God's people. The psalter served as a Jewish hymnbook, and the New Testament records early church hymns.

In 1 Timothy 2:1,[5] Paul instructed the church to practice *corporate prayer.* Whether praying for one's nation and governmental leaders, the infirmed, the church's ministries, the lost, or for God's blessing on the service, every time God's people gather, they are to offer prayers.

In 2 Timothy 4:2,[6] Paul instructed Timothy to *preach the Word*, explaining and applying the Scriptures for God's people. The preached Word is one of the central recoveries of the Protestant Reformation, even affecting church architecture with the pulpit becoming the central feature of the worship center and the main course of the worship service.

Additionally, observing the ordinances is always welcome when an individual is ready for baptism or the church elects to celebrate the Lord's Supper. Moreover, the regulative principle does not preclude making announcements, greeting visitors, or collecting an offering, but it does so mindful of the worship service's flow and where such ancillary matters are best positioned.

Biblically Faithful, Practically Helpful

While the regulative principle helps ensure the worship service is biblical, it also brings many practical benefits. As a pastor, one will often be asked for special promotions, features, or emphases to be made in the worship service. Some of these are especially cringe-worthy, sure to distract from the worship service, if not downright unbiblical. If the congregation has a general awareness of why the church does what it does in the worship service, then the pastor can point to that standard as an objective criterion. This depersonalizes the

denial of the request and avoids the appearance of play-
ing favorites.

Practicing these four elements brings other benefits
as well, including keeping the church in the stream of
believers from previous generations. It also sets the worship service on higher ground—thus avoiding worship
wars—and it ensures a certain baseline quality and spiritual vitality in the service.

This does not preclude a Sunday-evening concert,
a Bible conference, or a service exclusively for prayer.
Rather, it means we might best think of those events as
concerts and conferences rather than as formal worship
services. We might also more intentionally guard the
integrity of corporate worship, especially when God's
people gather on Sunday morning.

Keys to Strengthen Your Worship Service

As we have seen, the pastor is the worship leader,
and he should construct the worship service, feeling the
weight of that accountability. Intentionality is the order
of the day. You must give careful attention to planning a
service that is faithful to Scripture, honoring of Christ,
and edifying for God's people. Consider these twelve
keys to strengthen your service:

1. *Focus on Christ.* From beginning to
   end, help your people focus on Christ.

He is why you have gathered and in whose name you have gathered. Your attendees may not even realize how desperate they are for Jesus, but He is the only satisfier of the human soul. From start to finish, give them Jesus.

2. *Saturate it with Scripture.* In addition to the formal reading of Scripture, look for other ways to incorporate God's Word into the service. Meditate on Scripture, sing Scripture, and pray Scripture. Open the service with a scriptural call to worship; conclude it with a scriptural benediction. Speak the Scriptures clearly. It is the only inerrant word the congregation will hear all day.

3. *Preach expositionally.* Solid exposition has carried along many otherwise poor services. There is just no replacing a steady diet of God's Word. Make sure your people know what to expect when you enter the pulpit. Over time, a strong pulpit will lead to a strong church—and stronger worship.

4. *Plan worship for those who can worship.* Remember, the church gathers to worship and scatters to evangelize.

While you should be attuned to guests and unbelievers who may be in attendance, design the service for God's people to worship God and be equipped in the process. This biblical model makes the service more enriching for your members. What is more, guests can better see and behold Christ and why He is worthy of worship.

5. *Sing with musical accompaniment, not vice versa.* Generally speaking, modern church architecture is designed more for stage presentation than corporate worship. Lighting, speaker systems, and acoustic panels, are all designed more for attendees to receive than to contribute, musically speaking. Encourage congregational singing by toning down the stage music. The worship leader's singing and musical accompaniment should facilitate congregational singing, not drown it out.

6. *Feature the ordinances.* Baptism and the Lord's Supper are to be celebrated until our Lord returns, and they are a cause for celebration. They are not an interruption to corporate worship;

they are an essential part of it. Try to avoid "tacking on" the ordinances around the margins of the service. Work to feature them, explain why they are important, and cultivate in your people a sense of celebration when the church observes them.

7. *Rein in technology.* I am not a curmudgeon on this point, but generally speaking, I believe less is more. The more you use videos and other visual and technological supports to prop up the service, the more your people will grow accustomed to—and dependent on—the same. Do not underestimate the power of the big four: Scripture reading, prayer, congregational singing, and preaching. As we have seen, they are essential.

8. *Use strategic silence.* In general, our culture dislikes silence. We tend to appreciate noise, and we fill our lives with music, podcasts, audiobooks, and the like. We even have "noise machines" to provide background noise. The same mentality can creep into our worship service. Don't let it. Silence can aid reflection, create space

for repentance, and elicit impromptu prayers from God's people. Don't underestimate the value of strategically doing nothing at certain points in the service.

9. *Declutter and simplify the order of worship.* Over time, churches tend to add items to their worship service that have no place in it. Often, the announcements and promotions run amuck, but more troubling, I have seen all sorts of strange activities and items slip into the service. Be careful to not add too much to the service, and be mindful when you do.

10. *Allow only church members to lead worship.* The choir is not intended to be a half-way house, and the praise team is not an outreach program. Building a relationship with those who lead will aid in determining fitness to lead. Having a worship leadership covenant, including writing out one's testimony, can aid the process.

11. *Be kid-friendly.* Some churches signal that children are not wanted in corporate worship. They herd kids out like cattle and all but state restless

children are not welcome. There are a host of good reasons why parents may elect to leave a child in nursery or send them to a children's program, but sensing from the leadership that children are not welcome in the service is not one of them. Kids can sit for hours at school and in front of the television, so most can sit for an hour through a worship service. Encourage families to worship together.

12. *Evaluate your worship regularly.* It is easy to fall into a routine and to mindlessly proceed in it. You and other church leaders should evaluate your worship services regularly. What is more, you might occasionally ask a friend or guest preacher to give you feedback on your service as well. Distractions, hindrances, or just poor practices can creep in and undermine what you are trying to accomplish in corporate worship. Be on the lookout for these things—and eliminate them.

In Conclusion

I once frequented a restaurant that had fabulous food but always seemed just a bit much. The steak, which was hard to beat on its own, always had an added sauce splattered on top or a garnishment protruding from it. The chef intended the additives to complement the meal, but they wound up distracting—and detracting—from it.

Sometimes we do the same thing in public worship. Our attempts to improve Christian worship may, in fact, distract from it. Often, less actually is more. There can be a beauty in simplicity. We would do well to de-clutter our worship services.

When it comes to the pastor as worship leader and embracing the regulative principle, I am not legalistic. I still facilitate an offering, greet visitors, and make announcements. But a broad recovery and commitment to these four elements, and pastoral intentionality from start to finish, might well revive our worship services.

Pastor, be intentional about your corporate worship services and privilege these four biblical aspects of worship. After all, whether you like it or not, you are the worship leader.

Chapter 10

Follow the Leader

The Minister and His Leadership

The history of the world is but the biography of great men,"[1] argued Thomas Carlyle, a proponent of what has come to be known as the "Great Man Theory of History." This theory suggests that the broader movements and contours of history all go back to the leadership of great individuals who exerted unique influence on their times. Whether Carlyle's theory ultimately proves true is debatable, but that certain individuals cast long shadows is not.

More than a cultural observation or historical phenomenon, this is a biblical reality. Repeatedly in Scripture, we see God providentially calling forth individuals for consequential kingdom tasks. People like Moses, Joshua, David, and Peter dot the biblical landscape. In fact, Hebrews 11, in many ways, is a biographical summation of the great lives of the Old Testament—mini-biographies, if you will. Throughout history, God, in His sovereign will, raises up leaders to fulfill His purposes in this world.

Even though God has entrusted me with a leadership position, I will confess, I have a love/hate relationship with leadership. Mind you, my reluctance is not with the call to lead, nor is it with the particular leadership opportunities God has given me; it is with what I refer to as the Leadership Industrial Complex.

The Irony of the Leadership Industrial Complex

Perhaps you have read about President Dwight D. Eisenhower's farewell address to the nation. In it, he warned the American people about the rise of what he dubbed the "Military Industrial Complex." In the address, he painted a potential future reality where manufacturing weaponry and supporting the military needs of the country would become such a massive financial and business reality that it would lead to a cycle of military adventurism in order to justify the expense and maintain the industry of producing and procuring weaponry.

At least in part, Eisenhower was right. America has become an arms-producing juggernaut, with a defense budget that approaches the combined totals of all other nations of the world. Undoubtedly, we are an arsenal of democracy.

In a similar but obviously less severe sense, the twenty-first century knows a leadership industrial complex. As a society, we are inundated with magazines, books, podcasts, conferences, and the like, on leadership. And there is a peculiar irony overlaying all of this: though our generation enjoys a surplus of leadership materials, we seem to have a dearth of leaders. We look to Washington, and so often, only see gridlock and sophomoric behavior. We find ourselves often criticizing our leaders, and sadly, more often than not, it is deserved.

In the broader society, whether it is in the fields of sports, entertainment, or business, we often see a stunning lack of leadership. And, of course, most tragic of all is in Christian ministry, where we often see ministers lose credibility through some moral failing or strategic blunder.

The additional twist of irony is that leadership, as a field of study, is a recent phenomenon. In times past, individuals—inside the church and out—like Martin Luther, Charles Spurgeon, Martin Luther King Jr., Abraham Lincoln, and Winston Churchill, all led heroically, making lasting decisions of global impact without access to modern leadership theories or resources.

Leadership Matters

Lest you conclude I am minimizing leadership, stay with me. I am not. In fact, I am a leader and I cherish that divine assignment. God has called me to lead my family, Midwestern Seminary, and occasionally other ministry or life endeavors along the way. Personally, I find the task of leadership invigorating and life-giving. To borrow from Eric Liddell, when I lead, I sense God's pleasure. What is more, I even avail myself to many of the leadership materials that flood the market.

Moreover, we must always remember that leadership matters because it is a trickle-down phenomenon. If leadership is influence, then leaders are always influencing, for better or worse. Indeed, over time, followers tend to reflect their leaders.

More specifically, as the years pass by, congregations tend to resemble their pastors. If a pastor holds high the Scriptures, so will his flock. If the pastor is given to prayer, his church will trend that way. If the elders are evangelistic, the church will be more committed to the Great Commission.

Conversely, if a pastor is shallow in the Scriptures, do not expect to find much depth in the congregation. If spiritual coldness emanates from the pulpit, there will likely be a frigidness in the pew. If the pastor is known for coarseness, do not be surprised if coarse individuals saturate the congregation.

As you can see, the stakes are high. Because of this, it is imperative that you endeavor to follow Jesus well. You cannot lead well if you do not first follow Him well. As Paul tells the church at Corinth, "Be imitators of me, as I also am of Christ" (1 Cor. 11:1).

As a minister, there are four distinct realms of leadership that will matter most to you as you strive for faithfulness. Though each realm is important in its own right individually, I want to encourage you to focus on these in the following order.

Lead Yourself

When you read the biblical qualifications for the elder, there is a sense in which being a capable leader is absent from the list. But upon more careful reflection, it is assumed throughout the Pauline qualifications for ministry.

It is as though Paul is saying that to lead others in the church you must first lead yourself and your family well. In fact, he says that straightforwardly about the family, but the previous personal and moral qualifications for the elder are all exercises in self-discipline, or self-leadership.

This introduces a very basic, common-sense principle: for a leader to have followers, he must be followable. Central to this principle is personal credibility. In essence, how well you lead yourself will enhance or undermine your personal credibility. If you are spiritually dry or morally lax, that will undermine your spiritual credibility. If you are personally lazy, severely overweight, commonly tardy, or routinely drop balls, you will weaken your trustworthiness.

We often tend to think of leadership as taking heroic stands and delivering moving speeches. On occasion, that may well be a part of it. But for most of us, leadership consists of doing the little things right daily, being seen as mature, responsible, and on top of our affairs.

On the contrary, if others perceive that a dust cloud of chaos seems to follow you around, you will probably not inspire the type of confidence from others you need to lead them well. Therefore, the faithful pastor must practice self-discipline. You must hold yourself accountable. You must set personal goals and track your progress. Tell yourself "no" on occasion just to remind yourself that you can. As you demonstrate faithfulness in these small areas, others will follow you into greater ones.

Lead Your Family

Beyond yourself, your first realm (and priority) of leadership is your family. If you are single as you read this and do not perceive God is calling you to a life of singleness, then keep reading and prepare yourself, even now, to lead your future family well.

Recall that Paul says if one cannot manage his own household well, he cannot be trusted to manage the household of God (1 Tim. 3:4–5). This divine expectation should land on us as a warning, but also as an object lesson as to how leadership works.

Of particular note concerning leading your family, give special attention to these areas:

- *Spiritual Growth.* You should strive to be a disciple maker in your home, leading your children to Christ and encouraging them and your spouse toward godliness. Regularly practice family worship, facilitate spiritual conversations, set boundaries for spiritual and moral accountability, prioritize the Lord's day, and expose them to the sweetness of God's people.

- *Material Provision.* You lead your family well when you meet their needs. As Paul told Timothy, not to provide for one's own family is to be worse than an infidel (1 Tim. 5:8). Obviously, ministry may mean you live on a limited budget. At times, it has certainly meant that for me. Nonetheless, steward well what God has given you, and if added work is needed to meet your familial obligations, take it upon yourself to do just that.

- *Protection.* We want our children's morality to be inspired by the gospel and shaped by Scripture, being mindful to guard against legalistic, and especially nonbiblical expectations. Yet we should also be intentional to insulate them from activities, people, and technologies that would harm them. Monitor what movies they watch. Be guarded with their technology. Be skeptical of sleepovers. Keep an eye out for who they hang around at school. Be mindful of the music they listen to. Be careful about who they are alone with. The first step of stewarding a child's heart is to protect it.

- *General Orderliness.* When onlookers observe your family, they may not see a perfect one, but they should see a well-ordered one. We all have moments of chaos and even seasons of unhealthy busyness, but that should be the exception, not the norm. Work toward order, consistency, predictability, and stability. Fight against an overfull schedule and too many commitments. Prioritize meals, devotions, activities, worship, and trips together. Good things generally happen just by getting everyone in the room together. Even if there is not an activity planned, just be together.

The challenges involved in leading your family well are immense. There seem to be pitfalls lurking behind every corner, and unfortunately, when you fail to lead your family well, they are the ones who get the most bruised. As you seek to lead in a manner honoring to Christ in all aspects of life, be sure that you are particularly mindful about how you lead your family.

Lead Your Team

Though we touched on some of these items in chapter 6, I want to come back to leading your team and add further words of application, especially for ministry staff relationships.

First, choose the right team. When looking to hire staff members or elevate lay people, remember to keep the C's in mind. Look for their:

- Character: Who are they in their inner persons?

- Convictions: Do their beliefs rightly align with the church's?
- Compatibility: Do they fit well culturally with you, the team, and the church?
- Competency: Do they have the experience and/or gifting for the position?
- Communication: Do they communicate clearly and responsibly?
- Capabilities: Beyond their technical competency, what are their broader gifts?

Whatever you do when hiring, be patient and be thorough. Get plenty of references. Dig deep. Ask questions. Look for what is not on the résumé and listen for what the reference does not say. Above all, be patient. It is difficult work to hire the right person, but it's far more difficult to get rid of the wrong person.

Second, lead by example. Your team will be inspired by seeing your commitment and sacrifice. Lead them as you would want to be led, not how some unkind boss once led you. Nothing is more demoralizing for subordinates than to sense their commitment and sacrifice surpass that of their supervisors. This can sometimes happen in the local church if a staff member senses his effort and work ethic surpasses that of the senior pastor. A word of warning here: pastor, if you live in recreation mode, do not be surprised if, over time, your staff does as well.

Third, learn to communicate clearly. The most frequent interpersonal challenges arise from unclear communication. Do your best to communicate clearly and frequently, especially early in the relationship, and insist they do the same. I tell my team members that I do not want to learn about things through social media; I want to hear from them directly. Whether it is a matter of institutional importance or just personal update, they need to seek me out, not *vice versa*. Work to err in over-communicating, and require your team to do the same.

Fourth, remember that words matter. What you say matters, as does how you say it. If you are trying to be encouraging, use encouraging words. If you are trying to be corrective, use corrective words. Be detailed and specific in the feedback you provide. As a word of caution here, consider, once again, the seriousness with which the Bible describes the danger of our words. As James told us, the tongue can bring life, but it can also kill.

Fifth, work to be easy to follow. Some of this, as we have seen, will be due to your personal credibility. But also, you can do little things to enhance your follow-ability. Give people room to grow and the grace to do so. Communicate expectations clearly. Go out of your way to be supportive and encouraging. Seek their good. Remember, love is often spelled T.I.M.E.

Sixth, and finally, remember you want to hire people who make your heart smile when they walk into your office. You want team members who are not only competent, but who are also with you convictionally and attitudinally. You want to serve alongside individuals with whom you find a foundation of trust and mutual appreciation. Only then will you be best equipped to weather the interpersonal conflicts that come.

Lead Your Church

At this point, many resources on ministerial leadership go off the rails. Unfortunately, many churches and Christian leaders draw straight from corporate America. Yes, thanks to common grace, we might well find helpful leadership principles from sources outside of Scripture. But too many churches look to secular management theories and governance structures rather than to the Scriptures.

As the pastor, the most important fact to keep in mind is your own spiritual and moral credibility. We touched on this earlier when we reviewed leading yourself. When the pastor shows up, credibility needs to show up with him.

This is especially true when leading a congregation to make a major decision or change. If the pastor lacks personal credibility, the church likely will not follow him. He may get a token vote of support, but they will likely vote no with their feet and their pocketbooks.

As it relates to leading the church, consider the following three avenues of leadership the pastor enjoys. Use each of them wisely:

- *Lead with your voice.* Though the pulpit is for the sermon and the sermon is to be about the text, the pastor does enjoy unique influence over the people of God. They do look to him for his thoughts on pressing congregational matters and key issues confronting the church. Be careful not to turn the sermon into leadership pep talks, but do use your voice wisely to lead the church—especially in available church-wide venues not tied to the sermon.
- *Lead with your life.* If your life does not align with your words, both will be undermined. For instance, if you announce a particular ministry initiative is essential for the future of the church and you encourage all to participate, but you and your family sit it out, do not be surprised if the

initiative flounders—along with your
ministry.

- *Lead through your leaders.* This is an
essential component of your leadership. By gaining lay leaders' and ministry staff's buy-in, you will ensure
the new initiative starts with trac-
tion. You will also set loose dozens
of advocates, championing the new
cause and the one who's spearheading
it—you.

In Conclusion

While much more could be said about sound, biblical
leadership, I am confident that you have enough here to
reflect on. But I should leave you with one final word.
Leadership is not so much a destination you reach or
a threshold you cross, but a discipline to be cultivated
and a skill to be honed. With each passing year you will
likely grow in your leadership ability. Strive to do just
that.

Chapter 11

Reach the World

The Minister and the Great Commission

As a minister, there is no greater joy than leading a person to faith in Christ. That joy is compounded when you have the privilege of seeing that individual grow in their faith, maturing into useful ministry service.

I type this chapter after having enjoyed a most memorable evangelistic encounter a couple of weeks ago. We tend to forget most evangelistic encounters shortly after they occur, but I expect I will not soon forget this one.

My wife, Karen, and our oldest daughter, Anne-Marie, were taking our two yellow labs for an after-dinner walk. We found ourselves on a walking trail that runs parallel to Troost Avenue, a road that borders the Midwestern Seminary campus property.

As we walked along enjoying family small talk, a black SUV stopped in the middle of the road. The gentleman driving rolled down his window and blurted out, "Can you tell me how I can come to know Jesus?"

I stopped in my tracks and paused for a moment, wondering if what I heard was actually happening. The driver then said, "I've been looking all afternoon for someone who can tell me how to personally know Jesus Christ. I have been to several churches. They have offered me groceries and assistance. I told them I do not need food; I need to know Jesus." Then, once again, he said to me, "I am looking for someone who can tell me how to know Jesus. Can you help me?"

As you can imagine, I went from being surprised to being overjoyed. I smiled and said to the gentleman, whom I would soon know to call J.J., "Sir, I am exactly the man you have been looking for. Park your car and let's visit."

J.J. grabbed a Bible he had purchased that day, and we spent the next forty minutes flipping through the Gospel of John and the book of Romans. After unpacking the gospel and explaining what it means to follow Christ, J.J. repented of his sins and gave his life to Jesus.

In more than twenty years of ministry, I have never had an encounter quite like the one I had with J.J. The obvious providential hand of God in bringing our paths to cross, J.J.'s "what must I do to be saved" attitude, and the time we shared over Scripture all left me overjoyed. The entire scene was almost too good to be true. But it was true.

Though an encounter like mine with J.J. might be a rare occurrence, engaging in evangelism and missions ought not be. Pastors who preach the gospel are essential in God's plan to reach the nations. Moreover, evangelism and missions are at the heart of the call to ministry. After all, we are called to be ministers of the *gospel*.

How Shall They Hear?

Perhaps no passage more clearly sets forth God's plan for pastors than Romans 10:13–15 (NIV). In these verses, Paul unpacks God's plan to reach the world with the gospel. Notice the apostle Paul's airtight logic:

> "Everyone who calls on the name of the Lord will be saved." How, then, can they call on the one they have not believed in? And how can they believe in the one of whom they have not heard? And how can they hear without someone preaching to them? And how can anyone preach unless they are sent? As it is written: "How beautiful are the feet of those who bring good news!"

Paul's argument is stirring, but it is also inescapable. If you are a pastor, you are numbered among those who have the glorious responsibility to preach the good news. These verses should propel you forward in your ministry, and they should also keep you focused on the main thing in your ministry—preaching the gospel.

The Sovereignty of God and the Responsibility of Man

By nature, I am a goal-oriented person. I set goals for most every meaningful area of my life, I develop strategies and tactics to achieve those goals, and I measure my progress along the way. For better or worse, that same spirit has spilled over into my ministry, including my pastoral ministry.

Yet, that forward-leaning approach to life could potentially conflict with my own theological convictions, which are built upon the foundation of a high view of God, His sovereignty, and His providential work in our lives and ministry. More specifically, when it comes to evangelism, I believe in both the sovereignty of God and the responsibility of man. Spurgeon, as usual, said it well:

> That God predestines, and yet that man is responsible, are two facts that few can see clearly. They are believed to be inconsistent and contradictory, but they are not. The fault is in our weak judgment. Two truths cannot be contradictory to each other. If, then, I find taught in one

> part of the Bible that everything is fore-
> ordained, that is true; and I find that in
> another Scripture, that man is responsible
> for all his actions, that is true; and it is
> only my folly that leads me to imagine
> that these two truths can ever contradict
> each other. I do not believe they can ever
> be welded into one upon any earthly
> anvil, but they certainly shall be one in
> eternity. They are two lines that so nearly
> parallel, that the human mind which
> pursues them farthest will never discover
> that they converge, but they do converge,
> and they will meet somewhere in eternity,
> close to the throne of God, whence all
> truth doth spring.[1]

We should not make one truth supreme above the other; rather, we must be careful to maintain a faithful balance in our thinking, especially as it relates to our ministry goals.

Over the years, I arranged my ministry goals first around what I personally could accomplish. For instance, as a pastor, I had a goal of sharing my faith at least three times per week. Some weeks I shared my faith more, and some weeks less. But having that goal helped me stay evangelistically focused.

Beyond my personal evangelistic goals, I also set goals for our entire church family. Some of these goals would be public, and, together, we would strive toward them. Others would be private, a target I prayed God would enable us to hit. Such might include how many annual outreaches the church would undertake, how many doors the church would knock on, how many church members would take a mission trip, how large our missions offering might be, et cetera.

I would also typically set baptism and church attendance goals. These tended to be more in the "God, I am praying You will bless us with these ministry achievements" category than the congregationwide awareness category. You will have to work through these matters in accordance with your own convictions and conscience, but do not be so goal-driven that you are pressured to fabricate spiritual fruit that only God can produce.

Cooperative Missions

Southern Baptist ministers reading this book are likely aware that one of the distinctives of our work is cooperative missions. Simply put, this means we believe we can accomplish more together than we can as individuals and as lone churches. Historically, and currently, this partnership has most clearly been seen through the funding of missions, church planting, and theological education.

As Southern Baptists, we collectively support a few thousand overseas missionaries, fund hundreds of annual church plants, and subsidize the theological education of more than 20,000 students in our six seminaries. All of this, and more, is accomplished through churches giving to the Cooperative Program and occasional missions and ministry offerings.

As a Southern Baptist seminary president, I happily serve in an SBC leadership role, but my support for the Cooperative Program is not merely a "company line" I tow. I have seen its positive impact in my life and ministry, and I now daily see its impact on students training for ministry, missionaries being sent, and lives being saved. I believe in and love the Cooperative Program.

Whether you are Southern Baptist or not, I encourage you to be intentional about cooperative missions. You might be surprised by the synergistic ministry and mission opportunities available to you. These opportunities may strengthen you and your church more than you ever imagined.

Keys to Cultivating an Acts 1:8 Church

But refocusing a bit more narrowly, how can you create a mission mindedness within your own church? I think we receive a blueprint from our Savior Himself. When reflecting on the Great Commission, most minds race to Jesus' concluding words as recorded in each of the four Gospels. But Jesus' Great Commission is recorded for us a fifth time, in Acts 1:8. Reflect carefully on Jesus' words:

> "You will receive power when the Holy Spirit has come upon you; and you shall be My witnesses both in Jerusalem, and in all Judea and Samaria, and even to the remotest part of the earth."

Our Lord here depicts the church's Great Commission efforts as expanding outward, in sequential, subsequent realms of influence. You can think of your Jerusalem as the immediate context of your church, its town or city. Think of Judea and Samaria as the broader region and the neighboring regions. And, of course, the uttermost parts of the earth are more distant places and unreached peoples.

A healthy church needs to engage each of these spheres. To be honest, it can be difficult to adequately focus on these respective realms of ministry, much less to secure funds to engage them. Whether it is your personal preaching and evangelism or the church's engagement in the Great Commission, let me give you twelve thoughts to consider:

1. *Always persuade in the pulpit.* There is a saying in sports that great players "leave it all on the field," meaning

they fully expend themselves, holding nothing back. Great preachers do the same; they leave it all in the pulpit. As Richard Baxter said, "I preach as never sure to preach again, and as a dying man to dying men."[2] Preachers are to be beggars, imploring men and women to come to faith in Christ. We press people to repent and believe, we sing our Master's praises, and we uphold the beauty of Christ and the fleeting opportunity to follow Him.

2. *Never manipulate in the pulpit.* There is a fine line between persuasion and manipulation—be careful not to cross it. To persuade is to call people to follow Christ; to manipulate is to coax them there. To persuade is to point them to Jesus; to manipulate is to push them there. A wise preacher once said, "What it takes to get people to come to Christ is what it will take to keep them there." Let the Spirit draw people to Christ—He knows how to keep them there.

3. *Set evangelistic goals.* As we have already considered, we must maintain a balance between the sovereignty of

God and the responsibility of man in our lives and ministries. We must do the work He has called us to do; we must trust Him to do the work that only He can do. Nonetheless, I encourage you to set evangelistic goals for yourself and for your church. You might target how many doors you will knock on, how many times you will weekly share your faith, how many annual mission trips your church will take, or how large your missions offering will be. Although we are constantly dependent on the Lord for growth, we must sow the seed diligently.

4. *Personalize missions.* Don't leave missions in the abstract. Church members know we are to be missions-minded because of the Great Commission, and that we take missions offerings to support our missionaries. But it can all seem abstract, remote, and unrelatable. You will be amazed how personalizing your missions will inspire your people. Adopt a missionary family to support or an unreached people group to pray for. Perhaps you should

develop a specific ministry partner overseas and focus your energies on that particular place. You might want to occasionally Skype an overseas missionary and let them talk about God's work on the field. Whatever it takes, personalize missions.

5. *Prioritize the Cooperative Program.* We have already touched on this a moment ago, but I do want to encourage you to prioritize the Cooperative Program, or, for non-Southern Baptists, to prioritize ministry and mission work beyond your congregation. Churches too often become insular. An inward-focused church is an unhealthy one. Your people may not understand the importance of funding mission work beyond your own church and community. As the spiritual leader of the church, you, as the pastor, will be responsible to encourage them to do so.

6. *Lead mission trips.* The old adage is true: you go overseas to bless others; you return home as the one blessed. Few things impact one's spiritual life like getting dirty for Jesus. I have seen

countless laypeople transformed in their spiritual life simply by taking a mission trip. You will want to work with strategic partners (for Southern Baptists, likely the International Mission Board) and on-the-ground missionaries to ensure you are aiding their work and not distracting from it. Also, you want to make sure your church engages in a consequential, fruitful work. So be intentional, but also be faith-filled. As you enlist members to go with you, do not be surprised if they are not set on fire for the nations. And praise God if they are.

7. *Know your neighborhood.* Contemplating God's global work and the fulness of an Acts 1:8 commitment may be daunting, especially if your church is not particularly missions-minded. Start with your Jerusalem— your neighborhood. Work hard to build relationships with those nearest you. Even with neighboring unbelievers, try to position your church as the natural one for them to reach out to in their moment of need. Let them know

Jesus loves them—and that you and your church do as well.

8. *Do not be afraid of a program.* Programs often get a bad rap. As evangelicals, we have produced more than our fair share of evangelistic and ministry programs over the years. The push to more organic, less structured outreach and ministry, perhaps, has been an overcorrection. In a perfect world, everyone practices day-to-day evangelism, thus leaving no need for an evangelistic team or program. But in the real world, when "everyone" does it, often no one does it. In other words, do not be afraid to program outreach ministries, knock on doors, or facilitate Tuesday night visitation. A programmatic approach to evangelism is better than no evangelism at all.

9. *Incorporate testimonies into baptisms.* When you baptize, work with the new converts for them to be able to share their testimony in the baptistry. There are different ways to accomplish this. Perhaps the baptizing minister dialogs with the one being baptized, asking

them questions. Or perhaps the testimony is prerecorded and played on the screens right before the baptism. Also, remember family and friends often show up for a loved-one's baptism. Be strategic—you might see others come to Christ as a result. What is more, feature baptism. Make it central to your worship services. Remind people why it is important, and why it is worth celebrating.

10. *Do not make false converts.* Only God can make a convert, but man can make a false convert. Obviously, this most often happens unintentionally, and it can happen for a host of reasons. When evangelizing, be slow and take your time. Thoroughly unpack the gospel, repentance, and faith. Moreover, do not rush them to the baptistry. If they seem confused, reluctant, or spiritually suspect, they may well be. The contemporary church is filled with false converts. Let us do our part not to add to their number.

11. *Do not be too afraid of making false converts.* As serious as making a false

convert is, some pastors are so concerned about not making false converts that they never get around to making converts at all. Of course, as I have argued, only God can make a convert; but, humanly speaking, we are His agents. We represent Him. We speak for Him. We appeal, as though He were pleading through us for people to be made right with God. Do not be so fearful of drifting into manipulation that you forfeit all persuasion. Implore them on behalf of God to be reconciled to Him (2 Cor. 5:20).

12. *Money follows vision.* Lastly, when it comes to raising funds for missions and ministry initiatives, remember that money follows vision. Point your people to the urgency of the gospel and the priority of the Great Commission. Remind them of lostness, the needs of the nations, and the reality that sinners spend eternity separated from God in hell. If you are the pastor, you are also the pacesetter when it comes to evangelism and missions. Hold high the vision!

In Conclusion

This chapter may have been heavy at points, but I want to assure you there is no greater joy than seeing your church on mission and seeing lives transformed because of that mission. To this day, Karen and I have friends who came to faith in Christ in churches we served years, and even decades, ago. To see them continue to follow Christ, and, in some cases, serve in ministry, is a profound joy. Remember, Jesus came to save sinners, and He is using you to do the same.

Chapter 12

Weddings, Funerals, and Ordinations

The Minister and Officiating

B eing a pastor means you live a life of expectations. In fact, when you step into pastoral ministry, you step into the expectation zone. Some of these expectations are biblical and good, some not so much. Regardless, how you handle them will color your ministry in more positive or negative light, strengthening or weakening your position as you serve God's people.

One category of expectations is that of officiating weddings, funerals, and, on occasion, ordination services. By and large, these services will be glorious ministry opportunities. Time intensive, yes, but they are significant venues for you to minister the gospel and pastor the church the Lord has entrusted to you.

Yet, you want to be sure to get these moments right. Botching a wedding or funeral might not only disappoint the family to whom you are ministering, but it could also be a broader setback with your congregation.

Much is on the line for your ministry, and much is on the line by way of gospel opportunity as well.

Officiating Weddings

If not already, you will soon want to hammer out your convictions about marriage, remarriage, and the circumstances under which you are comfortable presiding over a wedding service. What is more, as you settle on these matters, you will want to clearly (yes, in writing) convey those convictions to a would-be place of ministry. This is key—make sure you are clear on this one!

Unfortunately, I have seen many failures in this regard. A new pastor has settled into his new place of service, with all seemingly going well, and then the child of a lay leader asks you to marry them. For one reason or another, the new pastor is uncomfortable officiating the ceremony. Perhaps the couple, or at least one of them, clearly is not following Christ, perhaps they are living together, or perhaps one or both of them are not involved in a local church in any meaningful way. You can pre-empt most of these congregational dustups by having a clear wedding policy, known and distributed in advance.

When you are approached about officiating a wedding, especially if it is by a couple you do not know well, give the inquirer your wedding policy. Have it typed and presentable. You can give it to them, then ask them to review the policy (*the* policy, not *your* policy), discuss it with one another, and circle back around if they desire to move forward.

Even if you still have significant concerns about the couple, you can agree to meet with them and talk through issues that have arisen. This will accomplish three things. First, it puts the burden on them. They will follow up with you if they are comfortable moving forward under your expectations. If not, you will likely not hear from them again. Second, it protects you from the accusation you shot them down without giving them a hearing. And third, it enables you to present the gospel to them and set forth what biblical marriage is.

On more than one occasion, I have initially had concerns about a couple, only to be able to lead one or both of them to Christ, and then, in due time, officiate the wedding. In fact, I challenge such couples with the reminder that marriage is a natural life juncture to take stock of their lives spiritually and to focus and prioritize themselves accordingly.

In the wedding ceremony itself, you will want to be familiar with three primary passages and build the service around one or more of them: Ephesians 5:22–33, Genesis 2:18–25, and Matthew 19:1–6. You can build a brief wedding sermon from any of these passages. Though you are speaking to the couple before you, you are also speaking beyond them, to all assembled for the special event.

The Service Itself

As to the wedding itself, here is a sample service. As I will point out below, you will definitely want a wedding coordinator, and I would discourage you from taking that upon yourself. Often in Protestant settings, the service will be based off the Anglican *Book of Common Prayer*. It is a beautiful, traditional service. Then again, in free church, evangelical settings, it is often more customized. For instance, a sample wedding service might look something like this:

- Grandmothers Escorted into the Sanctuary
- Mothers Escorted into the Sanctuary
- Candle Lighting
- Groom and Groomsmen Enter
- Bride's Processional into the Sanctuary
- Pastoral Prayer, Requesting God's Blessing on the Service and Couple
- Introduction: State the Purpose of Gathering, Marriage as a Picture of Christ and the Church, Present the Gospel
- Acknowledgment: Who Gives This Bride Away?
- Wedding Sermon: God's Design for Marriage (Genesis 2, Ephesians 5, Matthew 19)

- Exchanging of Vows
- Exchanging of Rings
- Lighting of the Unity Candle
- Pastoral Charge to the New Couple
- Presentation of the Married Couple (Ladies and gentlemen, I present to you . . .)
- Recessional
- Mothers Escorted out of the Sanctuary
- Grandmothers Escorted out of the Sanctuary

To Keep in Mind

1. *Have a printed wedding policy.* As stated above, this simple step will save you much time and, potentially, much heartache. Be clear in the policy about all the sticky issues: divorce and remarriage, living together, the contours of the service you officiate, etc. Let them argue with the policy, not with you personally. Even if they concur with the policy, do not immediately agree to perform the wedding. Visit with them in person and ferret out any remaining issues.

2. *Who is your wedding coordinator?*
   Though not a biblical conviction,
   practically speaking, having a wedding coordinator has been a nonnegotiable for me. By this, I do not
   mean the bride must pay an exorbitant
   amount for a professional coordinator. Rather, someone with experience
   must be designated to coordinate the
   wedding. Some churches, especially
   larger churches, have a designated
   wedding coordinator. If you show up
   at rehearsal without a wedding coordinator, chaos will ensue. The rehearsal
   will take twice as long as it should,
   and the service will likely resemble a
   traffic jam. Or, worse, they will expect
   the pastor (or your wife) to serve as
   wedding coordinator, which is not a
   winning position for you or them.

3. *Avoid serving the Lord's Supper.*
   As we've seen in chapter 8 titled
   "Administer the Ordinances," the
   ordinances are reserved for the church
   and should only be practiced by the
   gathered church; thus I do not administer the Lord's Supper in wedding services. One exception is for weddings

that take place at the conclusion of
the Sunday worship service, where
the congregation celebrates the wedding ceremony with the couple and
observes the Lord's Supper with them.

4. *Be aware of your church's convictions
   and expectations.* Some churches have
   long-established rules for weddings
   and receptions, written and unwritten.
   If you are new, you may be unaware of
   some of these rules. Does the church
   permit secular music to be played in
   the service? Is dancing permitted in
   the fellowship hall? What about alcohol? Do your best to clarify the written—and the unwritten—rules.

5. *Insist upon premarital counseling.*
   Within the wedding policy, you should
   insist upon premarital counseling. If
   you are not able to lead the premarital
   counseling sessions, see to it that your
   designee, or a known individual you
   are comfortable with, does. The main
   idea here is to teach the couple from
   Scripture the meaning of marriage
   and how it should function. You want
   to equip them for a healthy, biblically
   faithful marriage to follow.

Officiating Funerals

Funerals are much simpler than weddings and often have more ministry opportunities and gospel impact. Compared to a wedding service, my terms for officiating a funeral service are pretty minimal. My main concern is that I can plan the service to ensure it is God-honoring in content and specifically avoids secular or syncretistic components.

Typically, a funeral service should last no more than 35–40 minutes. A funeral service template may look something like this:

- Musical Prelude
- Opening Scripture Reading and Prayer
- Musical Solo or Congregational Singing
- Reading of the Clergy Card and Eulogy
- Music Solo or Congregational Singing
- Funeral Sermon
- Music Solo or Congregational Singing
- Concluding Prayer

As you can imagine, in funeral settings, emotions are often raw. The family is grieving, sometimes distanced family and friends regather, and often one or more of the bereaved have a profound sense of regret (they should

have reconciled with their parent, etc.). In these settings, the presiding minister will not only be leading the
service but may also have to be something of a referee
among the family. On occasion, this will put you in a
difficult position, so plan to think biblically, shepherd
carefully, and keep your cool.

Though less common than in previous generations,
graveside services are still customary in some parts of
the country. Graveside services are typically brief, intimate services with the family and close friends. I shoot
for ten to fifteen minutes max, and focus on prayer,
Scripture reading, and a few brief words of encouragement and hope.

To Keep in Mind

1. *Remember, the funeral director will
   be of tremendous assistance to you.*
   The funeral director will help you
   communicate with the family, understand their wishes, and coordinate the
   funeral's logistics as a whole. If you
   have questions, logistical or otherwise,
   you can lean on the funeral director
   for assistance. Early in my ministry,
   funeral directors were a huge help to
   me. If you minister in the same area
   for a number of years, you will likely

get to know the funeral directors near you. You should definitely cultivate those relationships.

2. *Get the clergy card.* The clergy card, or minister's card, will capture for you the basic facts regarding the life and death of the deceased. Typically, you will read the data it contains and perhaps other supplemental material during the time of eulogy. Pay close attention to the details contained therein and confirm their accuracy with a family member of the deceased. On a number of occasions, I have caught an error on the clergy card just in the nick of time. You do not want to get their name, birthdate, or some other essential fact wrong.

3. *Do not fake an intimate relationship with the deceased.* Of course, it is always preferred to have firsthand knowledge of the deceased, and often you will. However, when you find yourself leading a funeral for someone you did not know, that is okay too. I encourage you to meet with the family in advance and ask them questions about the deceased: what

was he like as a dad? What were her hobbies? How did he come to know Christ? What are some of your favorite memories of her? When the time comes for the funeral service, just say something like, "Though I didn't have the opportunity to know Mr. Smith in life, in recent days I have been blessed by getting to know him through his family and close friends. I have learned he was . . ."

4. *Meet with the family, but focus on one point of contact.* I encourage you to get with the family as soon as possible. If it is unclear who will preside over the funeral, it is even appropriate to volunteer, provided you would like to do it. You can say something like, "I am not sure what your family's plans are, but if I can lead the service or be of assistance in any way, I would be honored to do so." Again, approach the family early in order to give yourself the opportunity to minister to them, but also time to shape the funeral service in a God-honoring way. Many families will have no idea what should comprise a

funeral service and will look to you to inform it. Again, for simplicity, focus on one family member as your primary contact.

5. *Get the gospel in the service.* This has always been a nonnegotiable for me. I do not ask for permission; I just do it. If the family tries to waive you off from sharing the gospel, that might be a good sign that you are not the right man to officiate the service. If necessary, you can step down in a tasteful, but direct way.

6. *Be honest about the spiritual state of the deceased.* On this point, it is not that you say everything that could be said, but that you do not preach someone into heaven who everyone knows is not there. If the person was a saint, then referring to them as with Christ is certainly appropriate. If not, or if there is significant doubt, do not lose ministerial credibility or undermine the gospel by saying too much. You can always say, "If James could speak to you now, he would urge you to follow Christ." Regardless of where James is, that is what James would say.

7. *Avoid open microphones.* In some geographical and cultural contexts, it is common to open the floor for impromptu eulogies. I have seen that happen on a few occasions, and most every time the service goes off the rails. This seems to happen especially when a child loses a parent from whom they have been estranged. They suddenly want to say to them in death what they should have said in life. This is not a hill to die on; but, in general, I would encourage you to steer the family away from open microphones.

8. *Be brief at the graveside.* Graveside services are less common than they were a generation ago, but they still occur. As to the logistics, again, lean on the funeral director, but it is generally practiced that the minister will walk ahead of the casket and stand at the head of the casket. While at the graveside, be brief. A prayer of committal, a Scripture reading, and a few remarks will do. I usually shoot for ten minutes, perhaps briefer if there is inclement weather.

Officiating Ordination Services

Ordination itself, and ordination services, vary widely from denomination to denomination, and even from church to church within the same denomination. This is all the truer in Baptist and free-church traditions. In fact, some in church history have argued against ordination services altogether.

Given this variety, I will not spend much time on officiating ordination services, but I do want to give you a few key suggestions to keep in mind and, more importantly, propose potential questions for you to work through with a candidate for ordination.

The main point I want to drive home here is to treat the entire process with seriousness. Whether the service is for the office of deacon or elder, it is a high office. Too many churches announce, weeks in advance, a forthcoming ordination council on Sunday afternoon at 5:00 p.m., an ordination service at 6:00 p.m., and a reception for the ordained at 7:00 p.m. Obviously, when you have preannounced the service and the reception, you undermine the integrity of the preceding ordination council.

Over the years, I have participated in a couple of ordination councils where we simply could not move forward with ordination. As I recall, those men were either spiritually or theologically disqualified; they simply were not quite ready. On both counts, we delayed ordination for a period of time for growth and discipleship; then we happily moved forward. Because we had not preannounced an ordination service, there was no harm done to the individual. With that, let me point you to a few more items to remember.

To Keep in Mind

1. *Work from 1 Timothy.* Make sure the candidate for ordination is familiar with the accompanying passages of qualification from the Pastoral Epistles, especially 1 Timothy 3:1–7 for elders and 3:8–16 for deacons. Give the candidates plenty of time, in advance of the ordination council, to review their lives based on these verses. On more than one occasion, I have had individuals opt out of consideration after reflecting on God's standards for the offices. God is a high God, His offices are high offices, and His standards for those offices are high as well.

2. *Lay hands on no one hastily.* As Paul warned Timothy, we are not to rush to set someone apart for ministry, especially not a new convert. To do so does harm to the individual being ordained,

and, quite possibly, the church itself. When in doubt, take it slow.

3. *Be intentional about the ordination council.* The strength of the ordination council will directly correlate to the strength of the men who comprise it. Typically, ordination councils are comprised of other ordained men. Look for spiritually mature, biblically knowledgeable men—especially within the ranks of the ordained—to serve on the council.

4. *Use the ordination service as a teaching moment for the church.* Many in your congregation will have no idea what is taking place. Before your entire congregation, be sure to unpack the biblical offices of elder and deacon, why ordination services are special, and how the church should pray for the ones being set apart. Ordination services can be (and should be!) powerful services.

Potential Questions for Ordination Candidates

Over the years, I have worked from the questions below in ordination services. Obviously, whether the candidate is being considered for elder or deacon shapes the questioning process and the questions asked. As you will sense, this template is oriented toward ordaining one for pastoral ministry. For deacons, I have worked from this list, but condensed it to make it more appropriate for the office of the deacon.

Given time constraints, I have usually not worked through all of these questions with the potential ordinee. Rather, I give them these questions well in advance, so the candidate for ordination will be able to grow in these areas and be equipped to answer them.

Please answer each question clearly and concisely. When at all possible, give scriptural support for your answers.

PERTAINING TO YOUR CALL TO MINISTRY

1. Please share your conversion story. How certain are you of your salvation? Based upon what evidence do you have this certainty?

2. Explain your call to ministry. How certain are you of your call? Based upon what reasons do you have this certainty?

3. To what area of ministry do you sense the Lord calling you?

4. Discuss the qualifications for ministry found in 1 Timothy 3:1–7, and share how you feel you measure up with those standards.

5. Do those who know you best support your call to ministry? Why or why not?

6. In your mind, what sin would disqualify you from the ministry?

7. Under what circumstances would you abandon your call to ministry?

8. How have you been exercising your call to ministry in recent months/years?

9. Discuss the role your wife plays in your ministry. Include comments concerning how supportive she is of your calling.

10. In general terms, discuss your philosophy of ministry and by what adjectives you would like your ministry to be described.

SYSTEMATIC AND PRACTICAL THEOLOGY

1. Explain your views on the nature of Scripture. Specifically, state your understanding and belief concerning the following terminology:

- verbal, plenary inspiration

- inerrancy
- authority
- sufficiency
- canonicity
- current state of the canon
- expository preaching and the power of Scripture

2. With specific Scripture references, explain and defend your views of the following theological topics:

- the person and work of Christ
- the deity of the Holy Spirit
- the doctrine of the Trinity
- the exclusivity of the gospel
- the nature of the gospel (i.e., the lordship controversy, salvation by grace through faith)
- the reality of heaven and hell
- the appropriate means for assurance of salvation

ISSUES OF ECCLESIOLOGY

1. What is your understanding of church polity (i.e., the role of elders, deacons, pastor, congregation)?

2. What is your understanding of the role of women in the church?

3. What is a church ordinance, and in which church ordinances do you believe?

4. Explain your beliefs concerning church discipline and what the appropriate measures are for obstinate, unrepentant church members?

5. What is the current role of the Holy Spirit in the church?

6. Under what circumstances do you view a "church split" as being permissible?

PERSONAL, MORAL, AND ETHICAL ISSUES

1. What are your views on media, alcohol, tobacco, and profanity?

2. Are you personally engaged in any secret sin that would disqualify you from the ministry?

3. Is there any skeleton in your closet that, if it became public, would make this ordaining council regret having ordained you?

4. When did you last lead someone to Christ? Briefly walk through how you share the gospel and what you said.

5. What are your convictions about counseling people of the opposite sex?

6. What are your views on pressing cultural issues such as homosexuality, marriage and divorce, and abortion?

7. Under what grounds will you perform a marriage? Under what circumstances must you decline?

8. Share your convictions concerning financial stewardship. Specifically, share your thoughts on your personal giving to the church and personal financial indebtedness.

9. Under what terms, at the end of your life, would you consider yourself having faithfully fulfilled your call to the ministry?

In Conclusion

As you probably now sense, there is a lot more to weddings, funerals, or ordination services than most people realize. While it may be tempting to downplay the significance of weddings, funerals, or ordination services, do not forget that these are facets of the ministry that you have been called to perform or facilitate. As you enter these ministry contexts biblically informed and pastorally alert, you will be equipped to strengthen the church, minister to God's people, and extend the reach of the gospel.

Conclusion

Pastor, Stay Faithful

I will confess, I am not exactly sure what people mean when they talk of success in ministry, but whatever that is, I am sure that I want none of it.

I like to see the fruit of my ministry labors, as most every gospel minister does, and I even appreciate realizing quantifiable gains and hitting what might be considered pragmatic goals. But as for the world's conception of success, I want no part of it. Rather, with each passing year I simply long to finish faithfully.

Every time I read of a ministry flame out, I shake with fear. Every time I hear of someone falling in ministry for moral turpitude, I shudder and pray, "Lord, do not let that be me." I simply long to be known as faithful to God's call and faithful to the end.

That is my prayer for you as well, and that ambition was a contributing motivation for this book. Yes, throughout it we have considered awareness, disciplines, practices, and much more to strengthen your ministry. I suppose that this book might position you for a fruitful, more successful ministry in the eyes of some.

But as I challenge myself, I also challenge you. Above all else, strive for faithfulness. As we close this book, consider with me why staying faithful is so important.

First, you are called by God. Christ has given the church, in our age, "evangelists, pastors, and teachers, for the equipping of the saints for the work of service, to the building up of the body of Christ" (Eph. 4:11–12). One does not stroll into the ministry; one surrenders to it, receiving it as a weighty gift and calling. Pastors are those who have been set apart by God, have been called by His Spirit, and have submitted their lives to Him. This requires obedience not only to enter the ministry but to continue in it. So celebrate the calling, and in your submission to it, stay faithful.

Second, you are a minister of the Word. As we've seen, your one irreducible responsibility is to feed the sheep the Word of God. Paul stipulates that the pastor "must be able to teach," and he charged Timothy to "give attention to the public reading of Scripture, to exhortation and teaching" and to "preach the Word" (1 Tim. 3:2; 4:13; 2 Tim. 4:2). The pastor who faithfully discharges this responsibility does more than explain the Bible, he feeds the church—eternal souls—the bread of the eternal Word. Every Christian needs a steady intake of God's Word and a faithful pastor who rightly divides the Word weekly. This alone is worthy of high praise, so stay faithful in your ability to handle the Word.

Third, you are held to a higher level of accountability. The task of preaching and the responsibility of spiritual leadership bring a higher level of accountability upon you. It begins with the qualifications of the office, as outlined in 1 Timothy 3:1–7 and Titus 1:6–9, but it extends to other passages as well, including "Let not many of you become teachers, my brethren, knowing that as such we will incur a stricter judgment," and that congregations should "obey their leaders and submit to them, for they keep watch over your souls as those who will give an account" (James 3:1; Heb. 13:17). This fact is all the more daunting when you realize that pastors face more intense temptation. Satan targets those whose fall will do the most damage to the church and most sully God's glory. Therefore, we must live sober, Spirit-led lives. In your fitness for ministry, stay faithful.

Fourth, you confront more intense temptation. Peter tells us that Satan roams about as a roaring lion seeking those whom he may devour, and there is no one he enjoys devouring more than a Christian minister— especially an erstwhile faithful one (1 Pet. 5:8). When he does, he not only ruins a pastor and his ministry, he also destroys a family, disrupts a church, and discredits God's glory in that community. There simply is no sin like the sin of a clergyman, and there is no one Satan desires to bring down more than one whom God is using most fruitfully. Guard your heart. In your battle against temptation, stay faithful.

Fifth, you face unique pressures. There are days when pastors carry the weight of the world, and for reasons of confidentiality, all they can do is bottle it up. Whether it is a piercing word of criticism, a church member's scandalous sin, a draining counseling session, a rigorous day of sermon preparation, or just the operational challenges of most congregations, all of these burdens—and more—can mount up to make the strains of ministry seem at times nearly unbearable. In these times, stay firmly grounded in Christ and seek your strength in His faithfulness. In your dependence on God, stay faithful.

Sixth, you tend the flock of God. Pastors preach, lead, and fulfill a host of other responsibilities. When church members need prayer, counsel, or support, you stand in the gap for them. You bear their burdens. Such is the heart of a pastor, of one who loves his congregation. This is no easy task. Church members can be wayward, stubborn, and even rebellious. Thus, the pastor who loves and serves the flock is worthy of admiration. In your care for the sheep, stay faithful.

Pastor, this is you. This is your calling, your work, and your reward. As you honor God and strengthen His church, one day you will hear, "Well done, my good and faithful servant." Lord, let it be. Stay faithful.

NOTES

Series Preface

1. Carl F. H. Henry, quoted in Lewis Drummond, *Spurgeon: Prince of Preachers*, 3rd ed. (Grand Rapids, MI: Kregal, 1992), 11.

Introduction: Why I Admire Pastors

1. Theodore Roosevelt and Brian M. Thomsen, *The Man in the Arena: The Selected Writings of Theodore Roosevelt: A Reader* (New York: Forge, 2003), 5.

Chapter 1: Set Apart by God

1. I have written extensively on this topic in my book *Discerning Your Call to Ministry*, and I point you there for a fuller treatment on these matters.

2. Charles Spurgeon, *Lectures to My Students* (Grand Rapids, MI: Zondervan, 1979), 26.

3. Charles Bridges, *The Christian Ministry* (Edinburgh: Banner of Truth, 1958), 4–5.

Chapter 2: Preach the Word

1. Jason K. Allen, *Letters to My Students, Volume 1: On Preaching.* (Nashville, TN: B&H Publishing, 2019).

2. John Stott, *The Message of 2 Timothy: Guard the Gospel* (Downers Grove, IL: IVP Academic, 1984), 107.

3. John MacArthur, *2 Timothy*, MacArthur New Testament Commentary Series (Chicago: Moody, 1995), 177.

Chapter 3: Prepare the Sermon

1. Charles Bridges, *The Christian Ministry* (Edinburgh: Banner of Truth, 1958), 194.

2. "But we will devote ourselves to prayer and to the ministry of the word."

3. "An overseer, then, must be above reproach, the husband of one wife, temperate, prudent, respectable, hospitable, *able to teach*" (emphasis added).

4. I've written on interpretation and sermon preparation more extensively in *Letters to My Students, Volume 1: On Preaching* (Nashville, TN: B&H Publishing, 2019).

5. Vance Havner, *Peace in the Valley* (Shoals, IN: Kingsley Press, 2018), 7.

6. For more help on how to do this well, see *Letters to My Students, Volume 1: On Preaching.*

Chapter 6: Raising Up Leaders in Your Church

1. Charles de Gaulle, https://www.goodreads.com/quotes/431075-the-cemeteries-are-full-of-indispensable-men.

2. F. F. Bruce, *Commentary on the Book of Acts* (Grand Rapids, MI: Eerdmans, 1970), 415.

3. Timothy Z. Witmer, *The Shepherd Leader: Achieving Effective Shepherding in Your Church* (Phillipsburg, NJ: P&R Publishing, 2010), 43–44.

Chapter 7: Membership Matters

1. You can learn more about 9Marks at https://www.9marks.org.

2. Jonathan Leeman, *Don't Fire Your Church Members: The Case for Congregationalism* (Nashville, TN: B&H Academic, 2016), 100.

3. Ibid., 113.

Chapter 8: Administer the Ordinances

1. To quote Shawn Wright, "Some 'footwashing Baptists' over the years have considered footwashing to be a third ordinance based on Jesus' example in John 13. They have always been a minority for good reason. Jesus does not say washing feet is a portrayal of the gospel, nor does he tell his disciples to wash feet until he returns" (Shawn Wright, "Five Preliminary Issues for Understanding the Ordinances" in Mark Dever and Jonathan Leeman, eds, *Baptist Foundations: Church Government for an Anti-Institutional Age* [Nashville, TN: B&H Publishing, 2015], 88).

2. You can read the full *The Baptist Faith and Message 2000* here: http://www.sbc.net/bfm2000/bfm2000.asp.

3. Bobby Jamieson, *Going Public: Why Baptism Is Required for Church Membership* (Nashville, TN: B&H Academic, 2015), 40.

4. Robert Stein argues, "In the New Testament, conversion involves five integrally related components or aspects, all of which took place at the same time, usually on the same day. These five components are repentance, faith, and confession by the individual, regeneration, or the giving of the Holy Spirit by God, and baptism by representatives of the Christian community" (Robert H. Stein, "Baptism and Becoming a Christian in the New Testament," in *Southern Baptist Journal of Theology* 2, no. 1 [1998]: 6). Stein goes on to argue that a first-century Christian could have referred to their conversion to Christ by using any one of these components (Ibid., 12–13).

Chapter 9: Lead Worship

1. Nick Needham, "Worship Through the Ages," in *Give Praise to God: A Vision for Reforming Worship: Celebrating*

the Legacy of James Montgomery Boice, ed. Phillip Graham Derek Ryken, W. H. Thomas, and J. Ligon Duncan III (Phillipsburg, NJ: P&R Publishing, 2011), 409.

2. Gregg Allison, *A History of Worship* (Grand Rapids, MI: Zondervan Academic, 2012).

3. "Speaking to one another in psalms and hymns and spiritual songs, singing and making melody with your heart to the Lord" (Eph. 5:19).

4. "Let the word of Christ richly dwell within you, with all wisdom teaching and admonishing one another with psalms and hymns and spiritual songs, singing with thankfulness in your hearts to God" (Col. 3:16).

5. "First of all, then, I urge that entreaties and prayers, petitions and thanksgivings, be made on behalf of all men" (1 Tim. 2:1).

6. "Preach the word; be ready in season and out of season; reprove, rebuke, exhort, with great patience and instruction" (2 Tim. 4:2).

Chapter 10: Follow the Leader

1. Thomas Carlyle, *On Heroes, Hero-Worship, and the Heroic in History* (Berkeley, CA: University of California Press, 1993), 26.

Chapter 11: Reach the World

1. Charles Spurgeon, "Sovereign Grace and Man's Responsibility," *New Park Street Pulpit, Vol. 4* (Grand Rapids, MI: Zondervan), 338.

2. Richard Baxter, *The Poetical Fragments of Richard Baxter* (London: W. Pickering, 1821), 35.

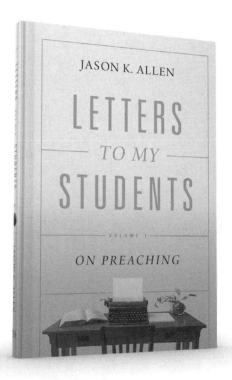